negotiating
environment
and ## science

negotiating
environment
and science

An Insider's View of
International Agreements,
from Driftnets to the
Space Station

Richard J. Smith

RFF PRESS
RESOURCES FOR THE FUTURE

New York • London

First published in 2009 by RFF Press, an imprint of Earthscan

For a full list of publications please contact:
Earthscan
2 Park Square, Milton Park, Abingdon, Oxon OX14
4RN 711 Third Avenue, New York, NY 10017

Earthscan is an imprint of the Taylor & Francis Group, an informa business

Library of Congress Cataloging-in-Publication Data
Smith, Richard J., 1932-Negotiating environment and science: an insider's view of international agreements, from driftnets to the space station / Richard J. Smith.
  p. cm.
ISBN 978-1-933115-70-2 (cloth : alk. paper)
1. Environmental law, International. I. Title.
  K3585.S62 2009
  344.04'6--dc22

                                              2008053674

Copyediting: Sally Atwater and Kristin Hunter; text design: Naylor Design, Inc.; text composition and jacket design: Ellen A. Davey; and marketing: Andrea Titus.

The findings, interpretations, and conclusions offered in this publication are those of the author. They do not necessarily represent the views of the U.S. Department of State and do not represent the views of Resources for the Future, its directors, or its officers.

The geographical boundaries and titles depicted in this publication, whether in maps, other illustrations, or text, do not imply any judgment or opinion about the legal status of a territory on the part of Resources for the Future.

978-1-933115-70-2 (hbk)
978-0-415-50548-2 (pbk)

About Resources for the Future *and* RFF Press

Resources for the Future (RFF) improves environmental and natural resource policymaking worldwide through independent social science research of the highest caliber. Founded in 1952, RFF pioneered the application of economics as a tool for developing more effective policy about the use and conservation of natural resources. Its scholars continue to employ social science methods to analyze critical issues concerning pollution control, energy policy, land and water use, hazardous waste, climate change, biodiversity, and the environmental challenges of developing countries.

RFF Press supports the mission of RFF by publishing book-length works that present a broad range of approaches to the study of natural resources and the environment. Its authors and editors include RFF staff, researchers from the larger academic and policy communities, and journalists. Audiences for publications by RFF Press include all of the participants in the policymaking process—scholars, the media, advocacy groups, NGOs, professionals in business and government, and the public.

To Ann

contents

about the author

Richard J. Smith was the principal deputy assistant secretary in the U.S. Department of State's Bureau of Oceans and International Environmental and Scientific Affairs from 1985 to 1994. In 1989, President George H. W. Bush appointed him special negotiator with the personal rank of ambassador to work out an air quality agreement with Canada.

As deputy assistant secretary for finance and development in the Bureau of Economic and Business Affairs, Smith led U.S. delegations to the French-chaired Paris Club, which negotiated the restructure of the official debt of developing countries. In the mid-1970s, when he headed the State Department's Office of Investment Affairs, Smith was the chief U.S. negotiator of the 1976 OECD Declaration and Decisions on International Investment and Multinational Enterprises. Smith was director of the Office of Canadian Affairs in the State Department in the late 1970s and deputy chief of mission at the U.S. Embassy in Ottawa in the early 1980s. Earlier assignments included vice-consul at the U.S. consulate in Nagoya, Japan, and financial economist in the State Department's Office of Monetary Affairs. After his retirement from the Foreign Service in 1994, he continued work on global issues at the National Intelligence Council

The author is the recipient of numerous awards, including two presidential honors, the State Department's Distinguished Honor Award, and several Superior Honor Awards.

Smith received a master's degree in international relations from the University of Connecticut and another in economics from the University of Michigan. He spent four years in the U.S. Coast Guard, serving as navigator and operations officer on a cutter in the North Atlantic, and as commanding officer of a long-range aid to navigation (LORAN) station in Hokkaido, Japan.

foreword

A lot has changed in international relations since the Victorian era, when Lord Palmerston, British secretary of state for foreign affairs, presented with the first cablegram to be sent to a far-distant ambassador, reportedly exclaimed, "This will mean the end of diplomacy!"

While the British Empire eventually ended, diplomacy did not, and the nature of international relations has continued to evolve over the decades. When Dick Smith and I became junior officers in the U.S. Foreign Service early in the second half of the twentieth century, the surest route to an ambassadorship was as a political officer: analyzing and reporting on traditional themes directly related to national security, primarily on a bilateral basis with a given foreign nation—its politics, history, rivalries, personalities, alliances, military capabilities, and territorial aspirations.

As it happened, we both began our careers in the economics field, at a time when this once-arcane subject began to assume an increasingly paramount role in foreign relations. Growing networks of international commerce, complex issues of international finance and investment, and the aspirations of newly independent former colonies for economic development, all contributed to the new importance of economic issues in diplomacy.

But time does not stand still. Later in our careers, Dick and I coincidentally found ourselves engaged in an entirely new field of diplomacy. In the last quarter-century, scientific, technological, health, and environmental issues become increasingly critical on an international level. Diplomats engaging in these non-traditional negotiations have had to acquire knowledge in exotic subjects that Lord Palmerston or even George Marshall would never have dreamed of—from space travel to melting glaciers to feeding habits of marine species. For example, in the course of negotiating the original Montreal Protocol, I needed to acquire a degree of familiarity with atmospheric chemistry that would undoubtedly have astonished my high school science teachers.

This important book, engagingly written, analytically lucid, and politically frank, is written by a seasoned, pragmatic, and outstandingly successful modern diplomat—a real professional. Dick Smith describes and analyzes eight "post-modern" negotiations of the 1980s and 1990s. In seven of these, he personally led the U.S. negotiating team; in the other, he chaired the multilateral meetings that resulted in the conclusion of an agreement. The negotiations involved such varied subjects as stratospheric ozone, acid rain, oceans and fisheries, migratory caribou herds, and space research. As a principal deputy assistant secretary in the Department of State, Dick was also involved in a myriad of administrative and substantive responsibilities during this period. The very fact that he could successfully lead complicated bilateral and multilateral negotiations in a variety of scientific fields, and involving such formidable counterparts as, among others, Canada, Japan, and the Soviet Union, is itself a *tour de force*.

Dick draws aside the curtain of discretion and mystique, and explains and explores the workings of this new diplomacy. He describes in fascinating detail the scientific, economic, and political complexities and ambiguities; the techniques of negotiation; the twists and turns; and challenges, frustrations, and breakthroughs. The historical, political, and scientific context of each negotiation is very thoroughly presented. It is a refreshingly personal approach, written in a clear and anecdotal style, devoid of jargon or obscurity, and laced with astute insights on the personalities involved. Smith comes across as calm, skilled, and professional, yet modest, learning intricate new subjects in ever-changing situations. His description of the critical role and potential influence of the chairperson in multilateral negotiations is particularly insightful.

Among the case studies are interesting glimpses of how a diplomat must cope with domestic factors that can strongly influence the course of an international negotiation—including interagency rivalries between U.S. government departments, the congressional process, political figures with personal or ideological agendas, private industry, and the new element of nongovernmental organizations (NGOs) and special interest groups. Smith does not shrink from revealing how domestic political interventions, often based more on ideology than on science, can attempt to undermine the diplomat's carefully prepared negotiating plan. Dick Smith, with an occasional hint of wry humor, is diplomatically generous to the troublemakers—who are, more often than not, home-grown. (At least, compared with the domestic factions, the foreigners are generally polite!)

His book is also a refreshing antidote to more academic political science studies that attempt to deconstruct and analyze international negotiations as a "connect-the-numbers" process: just do "A," "B," and "C," and *voilà*, your negotiation will succeed. The practicing diplomat knows that the reality is more subtle and unpredictable, involving skills, experience, and yes, even serendipidity. The seasoned negotiator also learns that, somehow, *Fingerspitzengefüehl*—the instinct and flair engendered by experience—can often inspire "good luck" at a critical moment.

In sum, this book—informative, thorough, and entertaining—will provide unexpected insights to a wide audience, from the informed general reader to the student of international relations to the potential or practicing professional descendent of Lord Palmerston.

—*Richard E. Benedick*

Ambassador Richard E. Benedick has played a major role in global environmental affairs as chief U.S. negotiator and a principal architect of the 1987 Montreal Protocol on Substances that Deplete the Ozone Layer, and as special advisor to Secretaries-General of both the United Nations Conference on Environment and Development (Rio de Janeiro, 1992) and the International Conference on Population and Development (Cairo, 1994). He is the author of *Ozone Diplomacy: New Directions in Safeguarding the Planet.*

preface

From mid-1985 until I retired from the Foreign Service in 1994, I served as the principal deputy assistant secretary in the State Department's Bureau of Oceans and International Environmental and Scientific Affairs (OES). The principal deputy's duties included coordinating and supporting the work of the bureau's four other deputy assistant secretaries for environment and health, science, oceans and fisheries, and nuclear energy and nonproliferation.

My last years at the State Department witnessed a period of intense diplomatic activity involving science and the environment. As the Cold War came to an end, interest in arms control and other security-related agreements declined. International agreements on environmental and scientific issues became more pressing subjects of negotiation for the world community. Countries grew increasingly aware that transboundary and global environmental threats, such as acid rain and the deterioration of the ozone layer, required internationally negotiated solutions. Further, they recognized that major scientific ventures, such as the construction and operation of a permanently manned space station, would benefit from a cooperative international approach.

During that period, the workload of the functional deputies in OES increased sharply, and I was called on to lead negotiations dealing with issues in their different areas of responsibility.

My purpose in writing this book is to provide the story of eight negotiations as seen from the perspective of the U.S. negotiator. The history behind these negotiations is worth preserving. These eight were selected because they have features that will be of interest to those charged with similar responsibilities in the years to come.

Each chapter in this book (except the last one) is devoted to one negotiation and follows a similar format. First, the chapter presents some background on the issues and explains how they became the subject of an international negotiation. Then, it covers the development of the U.S. negotiating approach, the highlights of the negotiation itself, and (where appropriate) the subsequent effort to gain U.S. government acceptance of the negotiated text. I conclude each chapter with some discussion of what can be learned from that negotiation and why it turned out as it did.

Particular attention is paid to the internal dynamic on the U.S. side. This is where the U.S. negotiating strategy is shaped and mid-course corrections are made. The interplay among the members of the U.S. delegation is often more difficult and intense than the exchanges between the U.S. delegation and its foreign negotiating partners. The interagency procedures used for resolving conflicts among different parts of the U.S. government play an important role in most negotiations.

The eight issues covered in this book vary widely in character and content. I begin with the London agreement to amend the Montreal Protocol, which dealt with substances that deplete the stratospheric ozone layer. The second chapter depicts a conten-tious confrontation with Japan over driftnet fishing. I then take up two bilateral agreements with Canada: an air quality agree-ment that addressed the bitter dispute over acid rain that had clouded relations between Canada and the United States for more than a decade, and an understanding with Canada to cooperate in managing the world's largest transboundary caribou herd.

The fifth chapter describes negotiations that resulted in greatly expanded cooperation on basic science research with the USSR and its successor state, the Russian Federation. I then describe negotiations that led to an agreement with Canada, Japan, and western European countries to build and operate a permanently manned space station, one of the largest international cooperative projects ever attempted.

The seventh chapter covers the first meeting of the Conference on Security and Co-operation in Europe (CSCE) that addressed environmental issues. The meeting provided an opportunity to en-gage Communist countries in dealing with global environmental problems and obtain recognition of the importance of the right of environmentalists and their organizations to have access to information about the environment as well as have their views heard.

The eighth chapter examines my chairing of the final sessions of an international conference that resulted in an agreement to conserve the pollock stock in the central Bering Sea. It was seen as a landmark agreement between coastal and distant-water fishing states that set an important precedent for the management of shared fisheries in international waters.

I present these negotiations in roughly chronological order, but in reality they overlapped a great deal. In some cases, talks with our negotiating partners spanned a period of several years or even a decade. Although each called for a different approach, some common elements may provide useful precedents for future environment and science negotiations.

In the concluding chapter, I consider the lessons learned and make some generalizations about negotiating international environmental and scientific agreements. Finally, I draw some contrasts between these negotiations and how the United States approached an environmental negotiation that turned out to be problematic: the Kyoto Protocol to the United Nations Framework Convention on Climate Change, which addressed global warming.

My primary sources in writing this book were my own recollections, as well as notes that I kept and working papers produced at the time the negotiations took place. I also drew on contemporaneous communications in which I was involved—primarily letters and memos. (This was a pre-email era.) The Circular 175 Memoranda, which were prepared to describe the purposes of a proposed agreement and to seek State Department authorization to proceed with a negotiation, were useful sources in a number of instances. Importantly, these were supplemented by renewed current contacts with many members of my delegations for all eight of the negotiations.

It is a truism that no two people ever attend the same meeting. Despite my best efforts to recount the events surrounding these negotiations objectively, my retelling of them inevitably reflects my own point of view. I want to convey to the reader a sense of how it felt to be the U.S. negotiator of these agreements and to be charged with resolving the issues that arose in connection with them.

acknowledgments

No one conducts international negotiations or writes about them alone. Certainly, in my case, I had lots of help in doing both. Many members of my negotiating teams contributed greatly, not only to the success of the negotiations covered, but also to my efforts to reconstruct the stories surrounding them for this book. They are too numerous for me to mention them all, but they know who they are and how much I appreciate their help. One of the joys of writing this book has been the opportunity to get back in touch with many of these former colleagues.

Current and former State Department officials who provided valuable comments and suggestions include Rozanne Ridgway, Fred Bernthal, Buff Bohlen, Eileen Claussen, Josh Gilder, Chuck Cecil, Dan Reifsnyder, Avis Bohlen, David Balton, David Colson, Stetson Tinkham, Don Braibanti, Robert Ford, David Jones, Carl Stoiber, and Susan Biniaz. Sue Biniaz represented the State Department's Office of the Legal Adviser on most of my delegations, and her counsel was an important input in overcoming many of the difficulties that we encountered.

Special thanks go to Carl Stoiber for letting me include in the book some of the drawings that he did during discussions of these negotiations in OES staff meetings. His "Carltoons" raise the art of doodling to a whole new level.

Other present and past government officials who provided comments on early drafts included Hank Beasley of the National Marine Fisheries Service; NASA's Margaret Finerelli; John Gustafson, who represented EPA at the CSCE conference in Sofia; Marshall Jones from the Department of the Interior; and the National Science Foundation's Gerson Sher.

Academics who were helpful on various parts of the draft manuscript include Charles Doran, who heads the program on Canadian studies at The Johns Hopkins School of Advanced International Studies (SAIS); Charles Weiss, Georgetown University; Bryan Mignone, Brookings Institution; Patrick Hatcher, University of San Francisco; and David Goldston, the Woodrow Wilson School at Princeton University and American University.

I want especially to recognize the significant contributions made by Richard Benedick, former deputy assistant secretary of state for environment; Alan Hecht, director for sustainable development at EPA; and Scott Barrett, director of the international policy program at The Johns Hopkins University. Each reviewed the entire manuscript and made extensive and constructive comments.

During the period covered by this book, I served as principal deputy to four OES assistant secretaries in the State Department—John Negroponte, Fred Bernthal, Buff Bohlen, and Elinor Constable. I am grateful to all of them for their unstinting support and for letting me take enough time away from the day-to-day tasks involved in managing the bureau to lead these negotiations.

I also want to express my appreciation for the part played by Don Reisman, my publisher at RFF Press, and his outstanding staff. Don was enthusiastic about the project from the first time I proposed this book. His thoughtful chapter-by-chapter feedback as I wrote it greatly improved the final product.

My wife, Ann, read the first draft of the book and dealt sternly with my occasional tendency to lapse into long-winded bureaucratic prose, making the final text more readable. Also, in the course of helping me sort out the papers and notes that I brought with me into retirement, Ann was among the first to urge that I consider writing a book about these negotiations.

While many people contributed to whatever merit the book may have, they bear no responsibility for its shortcomings. Those are strictly on me.

chapter 1

Earth's Ozone Shield

The signing of the 1987 Montreal Protocol on Substances that Deplete the Ozone Layer was a pivotal event in the history of global environmental negotiations, and it established a process that remains an important precedent for dealing with international environmental problems. A substantial share of the credit for this achievement goes to the State Department's Richard Benedick, the chief U.S. negotiator of the protocol. Three years later, the parties to the protocol met in London to consider amendments and adjustments to the agreement reached in Montreal. By then, Benedick had gone on to a new assignment. I headed the U.S. delegation to the working group that prepared for the London meeting.

The Ozone Problem

Ozone, a reactive form of oxygen composed of three oxygen atoms, is an air pollutant and health hazard when found at ground level. In the stratosphere, from 6 to 30 miles above the Earth's surface, it is more benevolent, forming a thin layer that screens out substantial quantities of ultraviolet radiation. This radiation would otherwise have a devastating effect on life on Earth, causing greatly increased occurrences of skin cancers, eye cataracts, and compromised immune systems in humans, as well as damage to animal and plant life.

In a *New York Times* article (December 7, 1986), environmental correspondent Philip Shabecoff wrote about the destructive effect of chlorofluorocarbons (CFCs), an extremely stable class of chemicals, on the stratospheric ozone layer. He noted that a warning about CFCs had been issued more than a decade earlier by Professor Sherwood Rowland and Dr. Mario Molina, scientists at the University of California–Irvine. In the late 1970s, Canada, Norway, Sweden, and the United States had responded by banning some CFC propellants used in aerosols, such as those used for deodorants and hair sprays.[1]

By the time that they had been banned in those aerosols, however, CFCs had become widely used and highly valued in a broad range of applications, from refrigerants and medical inhalants to firefighting foam and solvents for the electronics industry. No adequate substitutes were yet available, and the production of CFCs continued to grow. According to Shabecoff, an Environmental Protection Agency (EPA) draft report estimated that between 1986 and 2074, ozone layer depletion could be responsible for 40 million skin cancers and 800,000 cancer deaths in the United States alone.[2]

A Bumpy Road to Montreal

When I arrived at the State Department's Bureau of Oceans and International Environmental and Scientific Affairs (OES) in August 1985, one of the highest-priority issues then faced by the bureau was the negotiation of a protocol to the Vienna Convention for the Protection of the Ozone Layer. The Vienna Convention was a framework treaty signed in March of that year by 20 nations, including the United States, plus the Commission of the European Communities (usually referred to as the European Commission). The protocol, by setting specific requirements for reducing the production and use of ozone-depleting chemicals, would go beyond the Vienna Convention's general call for action to protect human health and the environment against adverse effects resulting from modifications of the ozone layer.

The outlook for reaching agreement was mixed, at best. Although the parties to the Vienna Convention had made a commitment to negotiate the protocol, they had not found any common ground on specific control measures needed to limit the production and use of ozone-depleting chemicals. The scientific evidence for damage to the ozone layer was not conclusive, and the CFC industry, represented by the Alliance for Responsible CFC Policy, was not yet convinced of the need for international controls. Also, senior officials at the Department of the Interior, the Office of Management and Budget, and the Office of Science and Technology Policy in the White House were skeptical of the need for an international control regime.

In its concern for controlling CFCs, Congress was ahead of the executive branch. With Senators Al Gore and Tim Wirth taking the lead, there was the prospect of unilateral congressional action should the international effort falter. Moreover, public opinion in the United States, prodded by environmental organizations, strongly favored taking action to control CFCs.

Several events at this juncture were to prove crucial. My colleague and friend Richard Benedick became the deputy assistant secretary for environment, health, and natural resources in OES and was designated by Secretary of State George Shultz to be the chief U.S. negotiator of the ozone protocol. Also, under Benedick's leadership, the State Department took on the task of heading an interagency effort to develop the U.S. position for the protocol negotiations.

The problem was to determine what level of control of CFCs would be justified by the science (as we understood it at the time) and be achievable, given the opposition to controls. Benedick argued that the nature of the chemistry involved was clear: these ozone-depleting substances would do unacceptable damage to the stratospheric ozone layer. Thus, in his view, we had to establish a control regime that was sufficiently stringent to require that production and consumption of CFCs and other ozone-depleting substances be eventually phased out and that substitutes for them be developed.

Benedick and I consulted as he sought to develop a negotiating strategy. While agreeing with him in principle, I counseled that we should proceed at a measured pace. What we were contemplating was phasing out a product essential to capital equipment worth billions of dollars. Moreover, we would be doing it for the sake of an unproved effect of an unseen gas in the stratosphere with consequences years in the future. He insisted—correctly, in the light of history—that given the threat to the ozone layer, we could not afford to proceed too slowly. He held that we should give an early and unmistakable signal to industry that the days of CFCs were numbered.

In November 1986, the interagency group that Benedick led reached agreement on negotiating guidelines for a treaty that would require an early freeze on CFC production at current levels, to be followed by a 20 percent cutback within four years. This was to be followed by a further cut of 30 percent within the following two to four years. Additional cuts were to be subject to subsequent periodic reviews and scientific assessments. The interagency group also approved a goal of eventually phasing out CFC use except for the most essential uses (such as medical inhalers), thereby achieving a 95 percent reduction in the production of CFCs.

The first two elements of that position, the CFC production freeze and the 20 percent cut, had largely been accepted as inevitable by both industry and the opponents of controls within the Reagan administration. Also, there were indications from Europe and Japan that a deal in that range was likely to be achievable. For example, these commitments could be met in Europe by simply following the U.S. lead in banning CFCs in aerosols.

Early in 1987, it became apparent that the strong U.S. position was gaining support. Senior officials in the U.S. government now raised objections to the negotiating guidelines, particularly the automatic second-stage 30 percent cut in CFC production. Secretary of the Interior Don Hodel and Bill Graham, Director of the White House's Office of Science and Technology Policy, complained that they had been out of the loop, even though both their organizations had been represented in the interagency group. Hodel and Graham claimed that the group's meetings in 1986 had been below their level of attention.

During the tough interagency battles that ensued, Benedick withstood high-level domestic pressures and personal attacks while continuing to argue the case abroad for a strong ozone protocol. Hodel and Graham attempted to force Benedick's removal as chief U.S. negotiator of an ozone protocol. As Benedick notes in his book on the subject, *Ozone Diplomacy*,[3] he had the unstinting support of Secretary Shultz as well as Deputy Secretary of State John Whitehead.

At one point during this intense bureaucratic struggle, the *Washington Post* reported that Interior Secretary Hodel had suggested at a White House meeting that protection from the sun in the form of hats, sunglasses, and sunscreens might be an alternative to measures to prevent the deterioration of the ozone layer.[4] Political cartoonists had fun with that. Herblock's cartoon in the *Washington Post* showed fish and birds wearing hats and dark glasses.[5] The opponents of CFC controls never fully recovered from the ridicule and derision. The press report cited Interior Department sources as saying that Hodel had proposed the hats and sunglasses alternative to give the president more options.[6]

Ultimately, the original U.S. negotiating position was approved intact, including the second-stage 30 percent cut, by a personal decision of President Reagan. The State Department and EPA, with strong support from the President's Council of Economic Advisors, had prevailed over the agencies advocating weaker controls— the Department of the Interior, the Office of Management and Budget, and the Office of Science and Technology Policy in the White House.

A Broad-Based Negotiating Strategy

Benedick's negotiating strategy involved pressing on all fronts. He engaged a U.S. chlorofluorocarbons industry that had been initially opposed to controls, working with it through meetings

—Copyright by the Herb Block Foundation

with individual industry representatives and through a series of workshops arranged by EPA. In a startling turnaround, the Alliance for Responsible CFC Policy, which represented about 500 U.S. producers and users of CFCs, changed its position: in September 1986, it announced its support for at least some international controls on CFCs and other related ozone-depleting substances. The industry was no doubt influenced by the growing scientific consensus on the critical consequences of damage to the ozone layer. Although substitutes for the manifold chemicals were still far from the market, chemists and engineers, particularly at DuPont, were now working intensely in researching and testing possible alternatives.

In the year leading up to the negotiations in Montreal, Benedick took advantage of the U.S. Information Agency's Worldnet satellite technology to hold a series of televised question-and-answer sessions on the problem of ozone layer deterioration. The programs were broadcast in more than 20 capitals in Europe, Japan, and Latin America. These broadcasts, conducted jointly with National Aeronautics and Space Administration scientist Robert Watson, had a noticeable effect on public opinion in Europe and Japan. The governments concerned had to take this into account while shaping their positions. Benedick also repeatedly visited capitals in Europe and Japan to hammer home the logic of our approach to those nations' officials. In doing so, he took full advantage of the discomfort of the public—particularly in Germany—with the European Community secretariat's initially more restrained attitude toward CFC controls. Through it all, he managed to monitor the contentious interagency process in Washington and ensured that our own position did not come unstuck.

The basic elements of the position that he fought for, both within the U.S. government and internationally, were intact when, in September 1987, representatives of 24 countries signed the Montreal Protocol on Substances that Deplete the Ozone Layer. The Montreal Protocol may appear inevitable in retrospect, but it certainly did not appear that way at the time. One needs to recall that when it was negotiated and signed, the evidence for significant ozone layer depletion was not yet irrefutable, and that a link between CFCs and a seasonal loss of ozone creating a "hole" in the stratospheric ozone layer over Antarctica had not yet been unequivocally established.

Preparing for London

By fall 1989, Benedick had moved on to an assignment as a senior fellow at the World Wildlife Fund and the Conservation Foundation. I had been following events related to the Montreal Protocol as part of my job in OES and was asked to assume leadership of the U.S. delegation to the working group negotiations preparing for the June 1990 meeting of the parties in London. Subsequently, in addition to my duties as the principal deputy in OES, I became acting deputy assistant secretary for environment, health, and natural resources, the job that he had held.

Much had changed since the Montreal Protocol was signed more than two years earlier. The evidence for the depletion of the ozone layer by man-made chemicals, more of which were being identified, was now much more compelling. The link between CFCs and the Antarctic ozone hole, and thus the need to identify and phase out ozone-depleting substances, was widely accepted. Most people were coming to realize that we would have to go beyond the existing control regime in the Montreal Protocol.

The First Meeting of the Parties to the Montreal Protocol took place in Helsinki in early May 1989. A new sense of urgency infused this meeting, which was attended by more than 80 countries, including the parties to the protocol and countries attending as observers. The participants acknowledged the mounting evidence of ozone layer depletion, as well as the need for funding to assist developing countries in making the transition away from ozone-depleting substances.

At Helsinki, the parties created an open working group—open to all parties, as well as interested nonparties—to prepare for the Second Meeting of the Parties to the Montreal Protocol, scheduled for London in June 1990. The working group was charged with negotiating proposals for amendments and adjustments to the protocol. The group was to take into account the work of four panels that the parties had established to assess the control measures provided for in the protocol, on scientific, environmental, technical, and economic grounds, respectively. The working group's proposals would then be considered at the meeting in London.

The four assessment panels completed their work in summer 1989. This peer-reviewed process involved more than 500 scientists and other experts and produced some 1,800 pages of findings. An integrated summary of the panels' conclusions, called the Synthesis Report, formed the basis for the working group's negotiations to prepare for the London meeting of the parties.

The working group began an intensive series of meetings in August 1989. Seven meetings of the working group, all well attended by parties and nonparties to the protocol, were held between then and the London meeting. By the end of 1989, 49 countries had ratified the Montreal Protocol. They included 18 developing countries, but not two of the major developing countries—China and India.

Funding for Developing Countries

A set of questions related to developing countries had come to the fore. How could more developing countries, particularly China and India, be encouraged to join the Montreal Protocol? If they joined, how would the costs of meeting their obligations be funded under the protocol? It was clear to me that although consensus on the control of ozone-depleting substances was within reach, an accommodation with the developing countries on the funding question was going to be much more difficult. Sensitive issues involving financial assistance and technology transfer would have to be resolved.

We made progress on the funding issue at the February 1990 meeting of the working group, held in Geneva. The developing countries accepted that their preference for a separate fund under the auspices of the United Nations Environment Programme (UNEP) was a nonstarter with the donor countries. The donor countries had a strong preference for using the World Bank to administer a fund on behalf of the parties to the protocol. Discussion centered on the mechanism that the parties might establish to oversee a fund within the World Bank. We also made progress in defining the kinds of expenditure by developing countries that would be covered by the fund.

At that meeting, EPA presented estimates of the fund's requirements in each of the first several years, based on country studies that it had conducted. The amounts needed in the initial years were relatively modest: slightly more than $200 million if China and India joined the Montreal Protocol and perhaps half that if they did not. The putative U.S. share, based on a UN assessment formula, would be 25 percent of that amount. The development of these estimates exemplifies the valuable contributions made by the EPA contingent in the U.S. delegation to the meetings of the working group. (EPA's senior representative was Eileen Claussen, chief of EPA's Office of Air and Radiation, who served as alternate head of the U.S. delegation.)

The Additionality Issue

The sticking point was the insistence by the developing countries that contributions to a Montreal Protocol fund be *in addition to all other development assistance*. The United States had resisted this so-called additionality concept in several other international contexts. Consistent with the position we had taken elsewhere, I balked at accepting additionality here. The United States was isolated in taking this position. The other delegations urged that we reflect on this issue with a view toward reconsidering our position before the next meeting of the working group.

I subsequently argued within the U.S. bureaucracy that we should accept the use of the term *additionality* and make clear for the record that we might interpret it differently. I argued that it was not really an operationally relevant concept. Aid levels are always in flux, and who can say what is additional to what? We were letting ourselves get distracted by an obscure North-South ideological point that had the potential to undermine the negotiation. The decision, in which White House Chief of Staff John Sununu was directly involved, went against me.

I was instructed to make a tough, uncompromising statement of our position at the May meeting of the working group. I was told not just to reject additionality but also to reject any fund that was separately financed, no matter where it was located and even if the fund did not receive financing provided in addition to all other assistance to developing countries. We would support a Montreal Protocol fund established within the World Bank, but its funding would have to come from a reallocation of Bank resources rather than from earmarked contributions from donors.

The predictable reaction to my statement was shock, outrage, and dismay. Delegation after delegation—developed and developing countries alike—accused the United States of undermining the Montreal Protocol. The World Bank representative at the meeting said that the Bank would not administer the fund without new and additional contributions. China and India stated that they would not join the Montreal Protocol if our position prevailed.

Claussen, EPA's representative on my delegation, expressed consternation that I had delivered the message in such a hard-line manner without leaving some hope that we could be brought along to a more forthcoming position. I felt that I had to deliver Sununu's views starkly so that others would recognize the seriousness of the situation and react accordingly.

Back in Washington, I sought to make the case that unless we changed our position on this issue, we were headed for a disaster in London: not only would the U.S. leadership role be lost, but also the viability of the Montreal Protocol would be jeopardized. We would be seen as the culprits. We would be alone on this issue, with no prospect of convincing any of the other participating countries of the rightness of our position. Further, I pointed out that our active participation in discussions of a separately funded Montreal Protocol fund at previous meetings of the working group had created reasonable expectations on the part of others that we would participate in such a fund. We would be frustrating those well-founded expectations, and our credibility as a negotiating partner would be at stake.

I would like to think that my arguments were persuasive, but most likely the firestorm of public, press, and congressional criticism had a greater effect on the White House. British Prime Minister Margaret Thatcher appealed directly to President George H. W. Bush to reconsider the U.S. position, as did representatives of the U.S. chemical industry. UNEP Executive Director Mustafa Tolba was reported in a June 13, 1990, *New York Times* article as saying that "if the industrialized countries failed to provide the economic and technical help required by the third-world nations, the 'global bargain' to protect the earth's environment would fall apart." The article also noted that legislation had been introduced in the U.S. Congress that would require the government to help the poorer countries protect the ozone layer.[7]

Just before the June meeting of the working group in London, which directly preceded the London meeting of the parties, Sununu issued a statement on behalf of the president. Although the statement stopped short of accepting the use of the term *additionality*, it said that we would agree to the establishment of a Montreal Protocol fund to which we would contribute, to be administered by the World Bank under the guidance of the parties to the protocol.[8]

In a June 22 op-ed piece in the *Christian Science Monitor,* Senator Claiborne Pell (Rhode Island), chair of the Senate Foreign Relations Committee, welcomed the Bush administration's reversal of its position. He was, however, scathing in his criticism of how the issue had been handled:

> Fortunately, and to its credit, the administration reversed this decision a week ago. But the way in which the original decision was made and then reversed highlights a serious flaw in the administration's international environmental policy formulation process. This flaw, which puts politics and ideology ahead of serious national interest in protecting the earth's environment, once again reinforced doubts about United States capacity for leadership in environmental diplomacy.[9]

Senator Pell went on to lament, "What we have seen is the dominance of political voices, emanating from the White House staff and the Office of Management and Budget, over the environmental policy experts in the Environmental Protection Agency and the Department of State."[10]

I was to make clear at the working group meeting that we were agreeing to a separately financed fund in view of specific, identifiable, and time-constrained needs of the developing-country parties to the protocol. Further, this was not to be considered a precedent for the establishment of such funds to deal with other global environmental problems, such as climate change. The potential problem of proliferating funds was a major concern of certain senior U.S. officials, including Sununu and Budget Director Richard Darman.

Edging toward Consensus

When I made my opening statement at the London working group meeting reflecting the changed U.S. position, the sense of relief that filled the room was palpable. There was still a lot of work to be done, but now a successful outcome seemed likely. Our conditions, including that the United States always be represented on the executive committee that would provide guidance on administration of the fund, made some uneasy; however, delegations were grateful for our shift in position and were ready to work with us on our requirements. In a welcome gesture, Canada offered Montreal as a permanent location for the executive committee and its secretariat.

I knew that many developing countries were determined to press in other forums for other environmental funds and would be reluctant to agree that they could not cite this fund as a precedent. To avoid a possible impasse on this issue, I said that the Montreal Protocol fund "does not prejudice any future arrangements,"[11] rather than has no "precedential nature."[12] This slightly more neutral language helped us get past what otherwise would have been a troublesome point.

The gratitude with which our shift in position was received reminded me of a passage from John Steinbeck's *Of Mice and Men*. The dim-witted Lennie is effusively grateful to his friend George for saving him from drowning in a lake, forgetting it was George who told him to jump into the lake in the first place. One delegate came to me and paraphrased a comment attributed to Churchill: "You know, the United States always does the right thing in the end—but only after exhausting every other alternative."

Closing the Deal

The London meeting of the parties that followed was held at the ministerial level. Bill Reilly, administrator of EPA, represented the United States, and I became a member of his delegation. Despite laboring many hours in day and night sessions, the working group had not been able to prepare a fully agreed text to present to the ministers for their consideration. Also, China and India had not yet indicated whether they were prepared to become parties to the protocol.

The ministerial meeting had some tense and uncertain moments, which were related primarily to how the issue of technology transfer to developing countries would be handled in the final text of revisions to the protocol. The developing countries wanted a commitment that they would receive needed transfers of technology on concessional terms. The developed countries were unable to make such a commitment because the relevant technology was in the hands of private companies. Agreement was finally reached on compromise language providing that the parties would take every practicable step to ensure that developing countries would receive the best available environmentally safe CFC substitutes and that related technologies would be expeditiously transferred. Further, the parties would seek to ensure that such technology transfers would occur under fair and most favorable conditions.

Ultimately, the ministerial meeting reached agreement largely along the lines that had been laid out by the working group. China and India accepted the compromise language on technology transfer and agreed to become parties to the protocol as amended, bringing the meeting to a successful conclusion.

In this meeting, as in the working group sessions that preceded it, UNEP Director Tolba played a strong personal role in helping the parties make the necessary compromises. He often met for extended periods with delegations seeking to work out differences, occasionally offering proposals of his own in an effort to break an impasse.

The London agreement strengthened the Montreal Protocol. It provided a move from a 50 percent reduction to a complete phaseout of CFCs by the year 2000. (Developing countries were granted up to 10 additional years to meet their target reductions.) Additional ozone-depleting substances—halons, methyl chloroform, and carbon tetrachloride—were added to the control regime. The parties also discussed the need for the eventual elimination of transitional substances, such as hydrochlorofluorocarbons, which have relatively low—but not insignificant—ozone depleting potential.

During the ministerial meeting, the developing countries had continued to resist having the Montreal Protocol fund established within the World Bank. They recognized the competence of the Bank and would expect its assistance in funding their transition to non-ozone-depleting chemicals, but they viewed the Bank as a creature of the developed-country donor nations. Eventually, it was agreed that the fund would operate directly under the authority of the parties and that its operations would be guided and monitored by the executive committee of the parties.

The provision on the financial mechanism contained in the London revisions called on the executive committee to discharge its tasks and responsibilities with the cooperation and assistance of the International Bank for Reconstruction and Development (the "World Bank" is the name that has come to be used for the five specialized agencies that it comprises, including the International Development Association), the United Nations Environment Programme, the United Nations Development Programme, or other appropriate agencies, depending on their areas of expertise.

The donor countries took comfort from the fact that the World Bank was in the best position to manage major projects in the developing countries. They anticipated that under this agreed formula, the Bank would be involved in overseeing most projects designed to assist the developing countries in transitioning away from ozone-depleting chemicals.

The "without prejudice" caveat with regard to other agreements was included in the provision on funding for developing countries contained in the final London revisions. This was helpful to the United States with respect to its opposition to additionality because it limited to this specific agreement any perceived deviation from its position on additionality. Also, the provision referred to contributions as being "additional to other financial transfers," but did not specify any expected amount of such other transfers. Therefore, the United States was not making a commitment that its contributions to the fund would be over and above any particular level of other foreign assistance.

The final document also included a significant trade sanction designed to encourage compliance with the protocol's control regime. This provision called on the parties to phase in a ban on trade in controlled ozone-depleting substances with countries that were not parties to the Montreal Protocol and were not otherwise complying with the control provisions of the protocol. That provision also said that the parties would determine the feasibility of banning or restricting the import of products produced using controlled substances, even if they did not contain the substances.

Thus, the text of the London Amendments and Adjustments to the Montreal Protocol on Substances that Deplete the Ozone Layer that the delegations adopted at the close of the meeting addressed the full range of outstanding issues. It led the major developing countries, including China and India, to become parties to the agreement. It initiated what came to be called the "Montreal Protocol process," which continued to respond to new information on the stratospheric ozone problem and to ensure that the necessary steps were taken to arrest and ultimately reverse deterioration of the ozone layer.

Reflections on a Landmark Negotiation

Some might argue the merit of holding out in an isolated, hard-line position until one almost causes the collapse of a negotiation, as we did in the final stages of the preparations for the London meeting on the issue of additionality. It is possible that such an approach can maximize what others are willing to pay in concessions to reach an agreement. But I would disagree. Too much goodwill and credibility gets lost in the process. In my experience, it is almost always better to work out the necessary compromises in a more collegial, give-and-take atmosphere.

In this instance, the United States, after being subjected to weeks of harsh criticism, appeared to be dragged reluctantly into the fold. Actually, the United States had long been in the vanguard on this issue and should have been receiving plaudits for its leadership.

A July 1990 *Washington Post* editorial about the London meeting noted, "Getting 92 governments to agree on anything, let alone on an environmental rule affecting dozens of industries, surely ranks as one of the more improbable feats of the season." The editorial went on to say, "The reasons for this extraordinary success deserve careful attention, for other kinds of environmental protection are going to require similar international consensus."[13]

The need to draw in and work closely with concerned industry groups and their congressional representatives, as well as with environmental groups, is certainly one of the principal lessons of these negotiations. Perhaps the central lesson is the need to design into global environmental agreements the flexibility to respond to new information as it arises. In acting before environmental damage becomes irreversible, we will usually be dealing with a substantial degree of uncertainty. We are not likely to get it right the first time. This was certainly the case in dealing with ozone layer deterioration. One of the greatest strengths of the Montreal Protocol is that it created a process of review and reconsideration— an approach that has allowed it to respond effectively to changing circumstances and new scientific evidence.

The negotiation of the Montreal Protocol and the London Amendments and Adjustments to it demonstrated the need for a new and closer relationship among scientists, policy makers, and diplomats. When facing potentially catastrophic global environmental threats, the world community of nations must act even in the context of considerable scientific uncertainty. We will be facing more challenges at the frontiers of science; if we are to realize the full potential of international environmental agreements, close collaboration between diplomats and scientists is more important than ever. The Montreal Protocol experience has shown us the way.

Subsequent meetings, starting with the 1992 meeting of the parties to the protocol in Copenhagen, added more substances to the control list and moved to earlier phaseout dates across the board. Because of the extremely long persistence of the CFCs already emitted into the atmosphere, it will be many decades before the stratospheric ozone layer repairs itself. However, its deterioration has been arrested, and the size of the cyclical Antarctic ozone hole has peaked. By fulfilling the hopes of its founders, the Montreal Protocol shows what can be accomplished when the world community comes together determined to deal with a complex and difficult global environmental problem. Its negotiation also demonstrated the importance of U.S. leadership in such efforts.

chapter 2
_____

The Driftnet Dilemma

W hen I joined OES in August 1985, the fisheries office in the
bureau alerted me to a serious and growing international
fisheries problem: Japan, the Republic of Korea (South Korea),
and Taiwan were sending out high-seas fishing fleets that were
using extremely long driftnets (12–30 miles in length). A driftnet
is generally about 8–15 meters in depth, with floats on the
top edge and weights on the bottom. It is allowed to drift for a
day, often overnight, before being retrieved and emptied of its
catch. Japan had taken the lead in developing these driftnets in
the late 1970s.

In 1979, Japan banned its vessels from driftnetting for squid
within 1,000 kilometers of its own coast, but at the same time
developed a squid driftnet fleet to operate in international waters.[1]
South Korea and Taiwan followed Japan's lead, also launching
high-seas driftnet fleets. By 1988, Japan's squid driftnet fleet
had grown to about 470 vessels. With the inclusion of the South
Korean and Taiwanese fleets, a total of about 800 such vessels
were engaged in driftnet fishing for squid in international waters.

Environmental organizations, particularly Greenpeace and
Earthtrust, sounded the alarm. These groups were using their
own vessels to track driftnet fleets, and they distributed pictures
of driftnet retrievals showing the wide variety of aquatic life

unintentionally caught by the squid fishery. These nontargeted species, or "bycatch," included dolphins, other marine mammals, and seabirds.

The environmental groups also learned that sometimes the driftnets were lost and not retrieved. These so-called ghost nets drifted freely for an extended period, greatly damaging the ocean ecology, before sinking to the ocean bottom. The environmentalists condemned driftnet fishing as a destructive and indiscriminate fishing technique and called for it to be banned.

The countries employing driftnets defended the practice and alleged that critics were basing their concerns on anecdotal and fragmentary evidence. For example, Japanese fisheries officials argued that their high-seas squid driftnet fleet was discriminating: the openings in their driftnets were sized so that the mature squid that they targeted would get partway through the net and then get stuck, but any smaller fish or other aquatic animals would pass through the net. Most of those that were larger would bounce off the net and avoid being caught. They acknowledged that some nontargeted species got entangled in their nets, but insisted that the numbers involved were not unacceptably large.

Dealing with the driftnet problem was especially difficult because these driftnet fleets operated entirely in international waters, outside the 200-mile "exclusive economic zone" (EEZ)[2] of any country. These fleets were not subject to regulation by any country other than their own because international law supports flag-state (country-of-origin) regulation of fishing fleets in international waters.

Developing a Strategy

The environmentalists were joined in their concern about driftnet fishing by U.S. fishermen, particularly Alaskan salmon fishermen, who feared that driftnets were intercepting salmon that originated in U.S. rivers before those salmon could return to their rivers of origin to spawn. International law recognizes that the country in whose rivers they originate has jurisdiction over the salmon throughout their migratory range, except when they are found in the EEZ of another country. By the mid-1980s, pressure was building to deal with the growing problem posed by the use of driftnets on the high seas.

Responding to that pressure, Congress enacted the Driftnet Impact Monitoring, Assessment, and Control Act of 1987. Known as the Driftnet Act, this legislation called on the Reagan administration to assess the effect of large-scale driftnet fisheries in the North Pacific Ocean. Significantly, the law also provided for the consideration of a ban on imports of fish from driftnet fishing countries that did not cooperate with the United States in its efforts to obtain information on driftnet fishing. This trade sanction would be imposed under provisions of the Pelly Amendment,[3] which authorizes the president to instruct the Treasury Department to impose a ban on the import of fish from foreign countries whose nationals are conducting fishing operations that minimize the effectiveness of an international fisheries conservation program.

Under the Driftnet Act, the president's consideration of such a sanction would be triggered if the secretary of commerce certified by June 29, 1989, that a country engaged in driftnet fishing had not cooperated with the United States in meeting the act's requirements. This firm deadline imparted a sense of urgency to all of us who were trying to resolve the driftnet problem.

OES, as the principal bureau in the State Department dealing with oceans and fisheries, had the responsibility for developing a strategy to address the driftnet problem. I believed that we had to begin by engaging in negotiations with Japan, which had initiated driftnet fishing and had by far the largest high-seas driftnet fleet. We would pursue an agreement that would put observers, including U.S. observers, on Japanese vessels to evaluate the damage being done by their driftnets.

We would also seek a commitment to increase the effectiveness of the enforcement of Japan's own driftnet fleet regulations, which included limitations on where the fleet could operate. One of our concerns was to ensure that their vessels did not stray outside their assigned areas into waters where they were more likely to intercept salmon that originated in U.S. rivers.

I was convinced that South Korea and Taiwan, with smaller fleets, would not agree to negotiate such an agreement until Japan had shown that it was willing to do so. Once an agreement had been reached with Japan, however, similar agreements with South Korea and Taiwan would no doubt quickly follow.

Japan did not want to appear to be responding to a threat of sanctions in U.S. legislation. Yet Japan wanted, if possible, to avoid a breakdown in the extensive fisheries relations between the two countries. If the United States banned the import of fish from Japan, Japan would feel compelled to counter with a ban on imports of fish from the United States. The result would be a significant deterioration of a fisheries relationship that substantially benefited both countries. Considering what was at stake, Japan, while stopping short of agreeing to begin negotiations on its squid driftnet fleet, reluctantly agreed by early 1989 to enter into preliminary talks with the United States concerning the fleet's operations.

The first decision that the U.S. side had to make was to determine who would lead the U.S. team in these talks and in the negotiations that we anticipated would follow. Ed Wolfe was the deputy assistant secretary in OES for oceans and fisheries and was a logical candidate to take on that job. However, he had a strained relationship with Kazuo Shima, councillor of the Japanese Fisheries Agency, who would be leading the Japanese side. (Kazuo Shima had an unusually blunt and brusque negotiating style.) Also, Wolfe was heavily engaged in other high-priority fisheries matters and would have been hard-pressed to devote the necessary time to the negotiation with Japan.

Wolfe and I agreed that it would be best if I headed the U.S. team in the driftnet talks and the subsequent negotiations. I was prepared to devote full time to the task and would have the benefit of a fresh start in dealing with Kazuo Shima. Also, I had had considerable experience in engaging with the Japanese, having served for three years in Japan, two as a Foreign Service Officer and one as an officer in the U.S. Coast Guard. In addition, I had taken some Japanese language training.

My initial task was to consolidate the U.S. position and establish what we hoped to accomplish. I used the U.S. advisers to the

International North Pacific Fisheries Commission (INPFC) as an advisory group for this negotiation.[4] Of the some 20 members of this group, the majority was Alaskan fishermen and representatives of Alaskan fisheries groups; the others represented similar interests in Oregon and Washington State.

Because the position of the Alaskan fisheries interests was critical, I made it a priority to build good relationships with fisheries officials in Alaska and with representatives of Alaskan fishermen and fish processors. I also worked closely with officials of the Commerce Department's National Marine Fisheries Service (NMFS) and with groups of concerned environmentalists.

Recognizing that many Alaskan fishermen were suspicious of the federal government, I traveled twice to Juneau in the second half of 1988 to convince them that I was committed to protecting their interests. On one of those trips, I appeared on a radio talk show beamed to fishermen in the outlying areas of Alaska, listening to their complaints and talking about what we should aim to achieve in a negotiation with Japan.

I also brought the INPFC advisers to the State Department for extensive talks on our negotiating strategy. Further, I spoke frequently with Robert Eisenbud, the minority chief counsel on the Senate Committee on Commerce, Science, and Transportation, who provided staff support to Senator Ted Stevens (Alaska) on fisheries matters.

I was struck by the fact that the value of U.S. fish exports to Japan was several times the value of our imports of fish from Japan. In 1988, U.S. fish exports to Japan were valued at $1.6 billion, compared with $500 million in imports from Japan. Thus, a breakdown of fishery trade between us—although it would hurt Japan—would hurt the United States even more. A resolution of the driftnet issue that did not involve imposing trade sanctions—if it could be found—would clearly be in the best interest of the United States.

The U.S. Atlantic Coast fisheries, which sold a substantial portion of their catch to Japan, would be particularly vulnerable to a failure of our negotiations with Japan. Lucy Sloan, a Washington lobbyist who represented fishermen and fish processors throughout New England and the mid-Atlantic states, kept me fully informed of their position. It was important to keep in mind the needs of this fishery constituency as well as those of the Alaska and Pacific Coast fishermen.

Another Stakeholder

Canada shared both the U.S. concern regarding the damage being done to oceanic ecosystems by high-seas driftnet fishing and our fear that these driftnets could be intercepting salmon that originated in North American rivers. Canada agreed with the developing U.S. strategy for addressing the problem and joined us in urging Japan to begin negotiations on an agreement dealing with its squid driftnet fleet. In those negotiations, we would seek agreement for an onboard observer program and enhanced enforcement. Such enforcement would include increased patrols by Japanese enforcement vessels, U.S. Coast Guard involvement to assist Japan in enforcing its regulations, and more severe penalties imposed by Japan on violators.

Although still balking at entering into direct negotiations, Japan did accept Canada's invitation to join it and the United States for trilateral consultations on issues related to the North Pacific salmon fishery and Japan's squid driftnet fishery. The meeting, at which I led the U.S. delegation, was held in Sidney, British Columbia, from February 27 to March 1, 1989.

The three countries, as founding members of INPFC, had for many years been dealing with issues related to salmon fishing in the North Pacific. Japan used this occasion to seek agreement, under the terms of INPFC, to convert its mother-ship salmon fishery to a land-based fishery that would operate directly from fishing ports in Japan. Because it was easier to monitor, Canada and the United States preferred that Japan use the mother-ship approach, in which the fishing boats brought their catch to a mother ship located within the salmon fishery. Nonetheless, Canada and the United States indicated that we would be prepared to agree to Japan's conversion to a land-based fishery under certain conditions, including the negotiation of a satisfactory squid driftnet agreement.

Japan resisted linkage between INPFC salmon matters, such as the use of a mother ship, and squid driftnet issues. However, by the end of the meeting, the Japanese accepted that the salmon mother-ship issue would have to be addressed at the same time as we reached agreement on the issues raised by the Driftnet Act.

The Beginning of Negotiations

Pierre Asselin (head of the Canadian delegation), Kazuo Shima, and I agreed that we would meet again in Tokyo, March 20–22, 1989. Asselin was deputy minister of the Canadian Department of Fisheries and Oceans. The purpose of the Tokyo meeting was to identify the major driftnet issues that needed to be resolved quickly if we were to avoid a crisis involving our North Pacific fisheries interests in 1989.

The March meeting in Tokyo was the first time that the Japanese were willing to engage in a serious exchange with Canada and the United States regarding the squid driftnet fleet. For example, the Japanese responded to a proposal that the United States had made the previous October on enforcement efforts on the driftnet fleet. Although the response had some positive elements, it did not go far enough to deal with our concerns.

The Japanese, moreover, showed no willingness to accept an observer program that would be adequate to provide reliable data on bycatch. I sensed that they were coming to fear that the kind of agreement we were insisting on would reveal the highly destructive nature of driftnet fishing and lead to its demise.

At this meeting, I expressed deep concern about some fisheries regulations that Japan had recently issued: these regulations would allow a northward expansion by two degrees (120 nautical miles) of the squid driftnet fishery during July and August 1989. I said that a significant increase in the incidental take of salmon originating in North American rivers might occur as a result of such a change. The Japanese responded that their scientists had determined that this change would not significantly increase the take of salmon. They added that they would monitor it closely, and if significant amounts of salmon were being taken, Japan would rescind the change. Kazuo Shima reminded me that the fishery was taking place entirely in international waters, where Japan, as the flag state, was responsible for its regulation. I reiterated our objection to the northward expansion of the fishery.

Deadline Pressures

We had made little progress at the March meeting in Tokyo. If a satisfactory agreement were not achieved before the end of June, the secretary of commerce would be required to certify that Japan had not cooperated with us in achieving the purposes of the Driftnet Act. The end of June would also bring the launching of Japan's squid driftnet fleet for the 1989 season, which, in the absence of an agreement, would proceed without observers or enhanced enforcement arrangements. We agreed to meet again in Washington, D.C., April 4–8, for a negotiating session that appeared likely to be the last opportunity to resolve our differences and avoid "certification" of Japan.

The April meeting, held at the State Department, was inconclusive. We made some progress, particularly on enforcement issues, which involved expanded monitoring activities by the U.S. Coast Guard and Japanese enforcement vessels. We were unable, however, to bridge our differences on an observer program. Also, Japan resisted employing automatic satellite transmitters on its driftnet vessels. These transponders would provide shore stations with real-time information on the positions of the vessels. This was important particularly to the Alaskan members of my delegation, who were convinced that Japanese driftnet vessels were going outside the area assigned by Japanese authorities and intercepting salmon originating in North American rivers.

Kazuo Shima said that it might be possible to persuade the Japanese squid driftnet fishery to implement a pilot program using transponders, but only if the United States agreed to the conversion of the Japanese mother-ship salmon fishery to a land-based fishery. I responded that Japan was trying "to put the cart before the horse." After Japan agreed to a satisfactory driftnet agreement, we would be prepared to favorably consider the conversion of the salmon fishery.

I told the Japanese delegation that one of our major requirements was that whatever arrangements we put in place for 1989 would be only a first step. The issues would have to be revisited in 1990. Japan had indicated its willingness to "exchange views" on follow-up measures in 1990, but this was not a strong enough commitment for us. I insisted that given the pilot nature of the 1989 programs under consideration, we had to receive a greater degree of assurance that we would build on those pilot programs in 1990.

We had clearly not made enough progress in this meeting to conclude a driftnet agreement, and time was running out. However, Japan, Canada, and the United States were not ready to accept failure of the negotiations without making one last effort to achieve agreement. We set up a final negotiating session to be held from April 27 to May 2 in Tokyo. In preparation for that meeting, I asked the fisheries scientists in NMFS and the Alaska state government to work together to prepare a detailed observer program that would go as far as possible toward the Japanese position that the program not be large and obtrusive while still generating statistically reliable data on the bycatch of the Japanese squid driftnet fishery.

Aware that the upcoming meeting in Tokyo was a make-or-break session, I went to it with a delegation of about 20, including many of my INPFC advisers and the fisheries scientists from NMFS and the state of Alaska. I wanted to be able to immediately respond to proposals across the full range of issues. Also, I wanted as many of the interested parties as possible present when the final compromises were made so that they would be on board should we achieve an agreement.

It was an intense negotiation with several late-night sessions. Once again, the negotiations on an expanded enforcement effort went relatively smoothly. We were able to agree to a significant increase of Japanese and U.S. enforcement-vessel coverage of the fishery, as well as an arrangement for having U.S. Coast Guard officers and Japanese fisheries enforcement officials assigned to each other's patrol vessels. Japan, however, continued to argue against the Canadian and U.S. proposal for an adequate observer program with Canadian and U.S. observers on board the vessels of the driftnet fleet, in addition to Japanese observers.

The use of position-finding transponders proved to be one of the most difficult issues. Kazuo Shima said that it was now too late for Japan to convert from a mother-ship to a land-based salmon fishery in 1989, even if Canada and the United States agreed that it could do so. This conversion had been linked by Japanese fishermen to their acceptance of a pilot program employing transponders. Without that conversion, the Japanese fishery industry felt that it would be getting no benefit in return for the burden of equipping vessels with transponders. Thus, Kazuo Shima took the position that it would now be impossible to implement such a pilot transponder program during the 1989 season for the squid driftnet fishery.

An Emerging Agreement

As we neared the scheduled end of the meeting on May 2, we held a final marathon negotiating session that lasted until 4 the following morning. The fisheries scientists on the three delegations succeeded in resolving their differences and putting together a draft agreement for an observer program. It was quite close to the proposal that the U.S. delegation had brought to the meeting, and the U.S. scientists believed that it would provide statistically valid information on the bycatch of the squid driftnet fleet.

In my experience, such all-night sessions are common as the parties to a negotiation approach its end and prepare to make their final concessions. (Negotiators want to show the constituencies that will be affected by an agreement that they resisted compromising their preferred positions until the very end.)

The Japanese were adamant that they would not accept a pilot transponder program on the squid driftnet fleet in 1989. They did agree, however, to test the transponders on U.S. and Japanese enforcement vessels in 1989 and—based on that experience—to consider employing such devices on squid driftnet vessels in 1990.

Importantly, the Japanese agreed that they would begin negotiations early in 1990 on expanded programs for that year's fishing season, based on the results of initial observer and enforcement programs in 1989. This commitment went well beyond their earlier expression of a willingness only to "exchange views" on such further steps in 1990.

I met with my delegation to review where matters stood and to hear their comments and advice. All of them accepted the judgment of our fisheries scientists that the observer program now on the table met our requirements for obtaining statistically reliable data on bycatch in the squid driftnet fleet. That program included an intensive component devoted to observing the take in the northern portion of the fishery to detect any increase in the interception of North American salmon, should it occur as a result of the northward expansion of the fishery during July and August.

All my delegation members also welcomed the significantly expanded enforcement effort that would take place under the agreement. However, several expressed disappointment (which I shared) that the Japanese were unwilling to install position-finding transponders on their squid driftnet vessels, which could be done at a cost of about $2,000 per vessel. We found it hard to accept that Japan would not even agree to undertake a pilot program testing their use on some portion of the squid driftnet fleet in 1989.

We were now at the end of the negotiating process. There was little time left before the 1989 squid driftnet fishing season would begin (less than two months hence) to get an agreement in place and implement the programs that we had been discussing. Without an agreement by June 29, the U.S. secretary of commerce would be required to certify Japan for not cooperating with us in achieving the purposes of the Driftnet Act. Trade sanctions would surely follow, and the Japanese squid driftnet fleet would set out to sea at the end of June without observers or an enhanced enforcement program. The fisheries relationship between the United States and Japan would deteriorate and become much more confrontational.

I put the case to my delegation. Should we reach an agreement based on what Japan was now prepared to accept? Or should we conclude that the attempt to negotiate a driftnet agreement had failed? I expressed my own view that what we could achieve was too valuable to let slip away. For the first time, we would be putting observers on a nonsalmon, high-seas fishing fleet. According to our own fisheries scientists, the observer program would provide reliable, statistically valid data on the bycatch of the squid driftnet fleet—and the collection of such data was the primary goal of the Driftnet Act.

I also put considerable weight on Japan's commitment to negotiate expanded observer, enforcement, and monitoring programs in 1990, including the use of position-finding transponders, based on the results obtained in 1989. We may not have achieved all our goals for 1989, but we had set up a process that would get us everything we needed in subsequent years. We had succeeded in pressing Japan to go well beyond its initial hard-line position. Moreover, I was convinced that the agreement we could now have would quickly prompt South Korea and Taiwan to agree to similar arrangements and ultimately lead to the end of driftnet fishing on the high seas.

There continued to be some grumbling, particularly about the lack of a 1989 pilot transponder program. However, everyone on my delegation—including the representatives of Alaskan fisheries interests—agreed that we should take what was now available in an agreement with Japan.

Japan maintained its position that as the flag state, it was solely responsible for regulating its high-seas squid driftnet fleet. We would therefore have to find some vehicle other than the usual international agreement to convey the understandings that we had reached. Thus, the terms on observation and enforcement were incorporated in letters from Kazuo Shima to me and James Brennan, assistant administrator for fisheries, NMFS, and from Kazuo Shima to Asselin, deputy minister of the Canadian

Department of Fisheries and Oceans. The letters were dated May 2, 1989.

As agreed, Brennan and I promptly responded with a letter stating that it was our belief that the programs for 1989, as described in Kazuo Shima's letters, together with the adequate observer and enforcement programs anticipated in 1990, would provide a basis for avoiding certification of Japan under the Driftnet Act. Kazuo Shima stated in one of his May 2 letters that should Japan be certified under the Driftnet Act, all the programs and measures described in his letters would be canceled, insofar as they related to the United States.

On May 5, I sent a letter to Clement Tillion, U.S. commissioner of the INPFC and one of my key advisers for the driftnet talks with Japan. (He had been unable to join the delegation for the Tokyo meeting.) As an Alaskan, he represented seafood processors, and it was critical that I have his full support for the understanding that we had reached with Japan. The letter contained a detailed description of the agreement, preceded by my evaluation of what had been accomplished:

> I am writing to inform you of our recent successful driftnet negotiations with Japan and Canada in Tokyo from April 27 to May 2. The understanding we reached in Tokyo will, I believe, help avoid a major breakdown in our overall fisheries relationship with Japan, establish a basis for developing a more cooperative atmosphere for 1989 and beyond, and greatly increase pressure to move Korea and Taiwan to accept U.S. scientific observers and to adopt enforcement measures for their high-seas driftnet fleets.

Opposition

In this instance, as is the case in most international agreements, it was up to the chief negotiator to take the lead in convincing Congress and senior executive branch officials that the negotiated agreement was in the best interest of the United States. On May 17, I was called to testify on the agreement before the Senate Commerce Committee.[5]

In my opening remarks at the hearing, which was chaired by Senator John Kerry (Massachusetts), I summarized the observer and enforcement programs on which we had achieved agreement as follows:

> The monitoring program calls for the placement of 32 Japanese, 9 U.S., and 5 Canadian observers on commercial driftnet vessels, including an extensive monitoring effort covering about 19 percent of the estimated net retrievals in the expanded northern boundary area during July and August.
>
> In addition, U.S. and Canadian observers will participate on one Japanese research vessel in the squid driftnet fishing area.
>
> With regard to enforcement, Japan has agreed to more than double its patrol vessel effort in the northern boundary of the squid fleet, from 265 vessel days in 1988 to 600 vessel days in 1989.
>
> Further, Japan will double its minimum port confinement penalties for violations of driftnet regulations and exchange with us enforcement observers on our respective patrol platforms [enforcement vessels] in this region.

I also noted that Japan had agreed to begin negotiations in early 1990 on expanded programs for the 1990 fishing season, based on the results of the 1989 programs. I emphasized my belief that a multiyear program was necessary to fully develop and implement these programs.

I was surprised when Henry Mitchell, one of the Alaskan INPFC advisers who had been with me at the final negotiating session in Tokyo, joined me at the witness table. I had not been told that I would be testifying with anyone else. Although Mitchell, who was executive director of the Bering Sea Fishermen's Association, had not objected to the agreement in Tokyo, I suspected that he was not at the hearing to be a supportive witness.

My suspicions were heightened when, before our testimony began, the committee was shown *Stripmining the Sea,* a film that had been made by the environmental group Earthtrust of Japanese vessels catching sea mammals and seabirds in their driftnets. Apparently, Mitchell was at the hearing to oppose the agreement reached in Tokyo as being too weak.

Senator Ted Stevens (Alaska) looked grim when he joined the senators waiting to question me, and I realized that I was likely to face some serious opposition from him as well. I made up my mind to push back hard, determined to defend the agreement with Japan as vigorously as possible. I did so realizing that this was not the response generally expected from a career public servant when confronted by an influential senior senator. However, I was convinced of the merits of this agreement and believed that its rejection would be severely damaging to U.S. interests. If it were to be rejected, I at least wanted to have done my utmost to avoid that result.

Senator Kerry began the first round of questions:

Kerry: I suppose perhaps an initial question is, apart from the sufficiency or insufficiency of the agreement as you see it, as a threshold question, should we be negotiating an agreement which involves transponders and observers or should we be looking for the phasing out and indeed the banning of this particular form of fishing?

Smith: Mr. Chairman, I do not think they are mutually exclusive. As a matter of fact, one of the reasons why it has been so difficult to get Japan to agree to such an extensive observer and enforcement package is that they recognize, and my [Japanese] counterpart told me that he fears, that the information that will be gathered by the three countries working together with their observers will lead to the beginning of the end of that driftnet fleet, and that concerns them.

I think that the things that are accomplished by this agreement, which gets us an order of magnitude more information than we have ever had before on these driftnet fleets, are the key to making the case that this method of fishing has to be looked at very seriously and perhaps ended.

Kerry: Do you believe the information [available without an observer program] is insufficient?

Smith: Yes. I think that what we need—in order to make the case effectively—is an extensive observer program. That is what the Driftnet Act called for. That is what we have negotiated.

The scientists who were with me—this included both NMFS

scientists and a scientist from the Marine Mammal Commission—are very pleased with the agreement. Basically, it represents the position that we had prepared.

The issue to focus on is that the position taken by these scientists is that you need to begin with a program of this kind. You cannot achieve all of the information you need on all of the fleets the first year.

What we have done is engaged Japan in a process. We have gotten a program which gets us more information than we have ever had before, and also commits Japan to consider further and broader programs in 1990. It is the path of cooperation.

I recognize the frustration and anger here. In fact, one of the advisors on my delegation—a person who represents a lot of Alaskan fisheries interests [not Henry Mitchell]—told me about this anger and this frustration when I first began this process. He said that you have got to remember, the people I represent really are not interested in agreements; they want a war. Well, that war is available, and we may end up with such an exchange in the trade area. But I would just submit that the first body bag in that war will carry the remains of the best observer and enforcement agreement we have ever had and information that is invaluable to us on the operation of those driftnet fleets.

Henry Mitchell countered that the agreement was inadequate and that the Japanese could control the data. At that point, I introduced for the record a cable on the agreement from our embassy in Tokyo, and I read to the committee the following quotes from it:

The agreement was achieved as a result of major concessions by the GOJ [government of Japan] and the Japanese fishing industries, departures from fiercely defended positions on freedom of the high seas and flag state independence. These concessions did not come easily for Japan...

The negotiators have since been criticized severely by dietmen [members of the Japanese parliament] and required to explain their posture. They explained that their objective was reestablishment of a constructive and non-confrontational framework for the long term fisheries relationship. They wanted to assure that Japan would not be certified under Pelly because of the Driftnet Act. This accomplished, they would work toward improvements in the high seas squid fishery (not necessarily a driftnet fishery forever).[6]

Turning to Mitchell's comments, I said, "Henry Mitchell made quite clear that his distrust of the Japanese runs very deep and comes from very long experience ... you should not make agreements with anybody you completely distrust. I am confident that they [Japan] are trying to extend the hand of cooperation here."

The next questioner was an obviously agitated Senator Stevens, who went on the attack:

> *Stevens:* I do not have much time. Let me ask you this. When did you represent to the Japanese that you would recommend to the President of the United States that we not follow the provisions of the Driftnet Impact Monitoring, Assessment, and Control Act, and that these measures would be sufficient to comply with that Act as far as the Japanese were concerned?

> *Smith:* I made clear that it was an ad referendum agreement, that I would bring it back, and as the negotiator bringing it back, that would be my argument. I might not prevail. That decision is made, of course, by the secretary of commerce.

> *Stevens:* But that is your position?

> *Smith:* My position is that this is a good agreement and I would hope that it is adequate to avoid the certification.

> *Stevens:* Well, as the principal sponsor of that act, I do not think you have read the Act.

> *Smith:* I have read the Act.

Senator Stevens, who was concerned that the Japanese driftnet fleet would be intercepting salmon that had originated in U.S. rivers, went on to accuse me of wanting to give "a bunch of pirates" a greater license out there on our fish than they had previously been granted within our 200-mile limit. My response rebutted that accusation and reiterated the value of the agreement:

> This agreement does not give them greater license for anything. It involves 1,400 observed hauls of the net, which will give us a

lot of information that will be of value to us. What is significant is that it is a precedent on a nonsalmon high-seas fleet where for the first time Japan has agreed to an observer and enforcement program.

Senator Stevens then asked, "Do you know what a squid looks like?" I paused before answering. As a U.S. Coast Guard officer, I had once served as commanding officer of a long-range aid to navigation (LORAN) station just outside Matsumae, a fishing village on the southwestern coast of Hokkaido, the northernmost of the main Japanese islands. During the squid-fishing season, the streets are lined with racks of drying squid. I decided that it would be counterproductive to pass on this information to Senator Stevens, replying simply, "Yes, I know what a squid looks like."

The senator from Alaska made clear that, in his judgment, the understanding with Japan should and would be rejected:

> *Stevens:* If the driftnet legislation is to be abandoned and not fulfilled, I think it would be the worst symbol that could happen as far as the environmental policies of the Bush administration.

> *Smith:* Well, there is obviously a difference of opinion. My view is that this agreement would set us on a cooperative path which would achieve the purposes of the Driftnet Act. That is why I brought it back. I mean, it may not prevail, but that is why I brought it back.

> *Stevens:* Well, when it is rejected, will you be the one to go back to the table again?

> *Smith:* No, no. We will give someone else that honor.

I was concerned that the hearing might be leaving the impression that the most interested parties, such as the Alaskan fisheries groups, opposed the agreement with Japan. To counter that impression, I interjected to make the point that the agreement had substantial support:

> *Smith:* If I could react just quickly, because I have been hearing from a lot of interests, including those in Alaska, that favor this agreement, too. The Alaska cold storage employers' group has written me a letter or has written a letter to Secretary Mosbacher.

There are two or three others that have. I have called all of the advisors of the INPFC advisory group, which advises me in this negotiation, and they are about 80 percent in favor of the agreement. There are several who are undecided and several who are against it, so it is not all on one side in terms of the affected interests of this agreement.

Stevens: I do not understand that last statement, Mr. Smith. I think I have talked to all the INPFC advisors within the last two months, the last three weeks as a matter of fact, and I have not found one who supports this agreement.

Smith: Let me provide you with a list. I have had conversations within the last day with virtually all of them, and I would be happy to provide your office with a list and the comments they made to me.

Stevens: I would like to have that, because I think maybe some of them ought not to be reappointed. They do not reflect our point of view.

After the hearing, I once again called my INPFC advisers to confirm their position on the understanding that we had reached with Japan. I was worried that given Senator Stevens's hostility, some of them might change their minds or ask me not to report their views to the senator. But my high regard for this tough-minded fisheries community went even higher when—to a person—they reiterated the views that they had given me a few days earlier and showed no reluctance to having me report their positions to Senator Stevens. A typical response was "Damn right, you can tell Ted Stevens where I stand."

In a letter dated May 18 to Eisenbud, the committee's minority chief counsel, who provided staff support to Senator Stevens, I reported the results of my calls. I had reached 19 INPFC advisers. Of that number, 6 indicated that they were still considering the matter and were not ready to say whether they favored going forward with the agreement. Of the remaining 13, 2 were opposed to the understandings reached and did not believe that they were adequate to justify withholding certification under the Driftnet Act. The 11 others believed that we were better off to proceed with the agreements negotiated and to seek to build on the 1989 programs in 1990 and beyond. Thus, as I summarized in my letter to Eisenbud, 11 of the 13 advisers (more than 80 percent) who had come to a decision were recommending that we proceed with the agreement as negotiated.

The End Game

It was now up to Secretary of Commerce Robert Mosbacher to decide whether to certify Japan as not cooperating in achieving the purposes of the Driftnet Act. Since returning from Tokyo, I had sought unsuccessfully to get an appointment to brief him on the understanding that we had reached with Japan. I noted, however, that Secretary Mosbacher did meet with Senate staffer Eisenbud, who represented Senator Stevens's views and, I assumed, argued in favor of certification of Japan.

The secretary of commerce received an array of letters from fisheries interests and members of Congress, representing constituencies on both the East and the West Coasts of the United States, supporting and opposing the understanding with Japan. The views of the powerful Senator Stevens carried considerable weight, particularly given the prominent role that he played on a wide range of fisheries matters of importance to the Commerce Department's NMFS. Alaska's other senator, Frank Murkowski, was also making his opposition to the agreement known to the secretaries of state and commerce.

There was no time left to resume negotiations with Japan before the June 29 deadline for making a decision regarding certification. Moreover, the Japanese had made clear that they would not agree to renew negotiations and would make no further concessions. If the understanding reached with the Japanese was rejected and they were certified, they would then proceed to fish with no agreement. Given those circumstances, Secretary Mosbacher asked Japan to reassert at a higher level its commitment to negotiate a broader observer program and accept transponders on the squid driftnet fleet in 1990.

Japan was not happy with this insistence that it repeat and elaborate on what it had already agreed to do. Nonetheless, to avoid a crisis in U.S.-Japanese relations, Hirohisa Tanaka, director general of the Fisheries Agency of Japan, wrote a letter dated June 26 to OES Assistant Secretary Frederick M. Bernthal and NMFS Administrator William E. Evans. The letter confirmed in more extensive language that it was Japan's intention to carry out expanded monitoring and observer programs, including the use of transponders, for the squid driftnet fleet in 1990. Significantly, Tanaka said that it was Japan's objective "to obtain statistically reliable data," which tracked language in the Driftnet Act.

Japanese Ambassador Nobuo Matsunaga wrote to Secretary Mosbacher and to Secretary of State James Baker giving comparable assurances, stating that Japan intended to cooperate with the United States on these programs through 1990 and beyond. We also sent a revised Smith-Brennan letter to Kazuo Shima that contained more explicit language on our expectations and received from him a response giving us the further assurances that we were seeking. Thus, without making any substantive change to the understandings that we had reached in Tokyo, we were able to provide some additional comfort to those who were skeptical of the agreement.

Anticipating these further assurances, Mosbacher announced on June 23, 1989, that the United States and Japan had reached agreement. He said, "This agreement achieves a real commitment, rather than a vague promise, that major advances in Japanese fleet monitoring and enforcement will take place on a multi-year basis." The announcement concluded, "The Driftnet Act of 1987 gave the commerce secretary until June 29 to reach an agreement. Without such an agreement, Japan could have been 'certified,' an action that could have led to an embargo of its fishery imports."[7]

Consequences of Agreement

Once the understanding with Japan was in place, South Korea and Taiwan were unable to resist the pressure to reach an understanding with us. They quickly agreed to undertake unprecedented observer and enforcement programs on their high-seas driftnet fleets. Although these agreements came too late for the programs to be implemented in 1989, they were reached soon enough to avoid certification under the Driftnet Act.

During the 1989 fishing season, the observer program undertaken pursuant to our understanding with Japan (the North Pacific Joint Observer Program) revealed that the driftnet fleets were indeed catching an appalling number of marine species not targeted by the fishery. The report of the joint observer program for 1989, which was issued on June 30, 1990, showed the results of 1,402 net retrievals that had been observed. The catch included 3,119,061 squid, 914 dolphins, 22 marine turtles, 9,173 seabirds, and 1,580,068 nontargeted fish, including 79 salmonids, 1,433,496 pomfrets, 59,060 albacore, 10,495 yellowtail, 7,155 skipjack, and 58,100 blue sharks.[8]

The huge take of nontargeted species documented by the 1989 observer program galvanized worldwide opposition to driftnet fishing. In 1990, the fleets of Japan, Korea, and Taiwan were subjected to extensive regulation and expanded observer and enforcement programs, including the installation of position-finding transponders on driftnet vessels. As a result, irrefutable scientific evidence was collected to back up the argument that driftnets were doing unacceptable damage to the marine environment.

With statistically valid data on the bycatch of the driftnet fleets now in hand, the United States and other countries stepped up their efforts to have the United Nations act against driftnet fishing. The nations of the South Pacific had already adopted the Tarawa Declaration calling for a ban on all driftnet operations in the South Pacific in June 1989. In November 1991, Earthtrust showed its new video on driftnet fishing, *Closing the Curtains of Death,* to UN delegations from many countries.

On December 20, 1991, the UN General Assembly adopted a resolution that called for a 50 percent reduction in driftnet operations by June 30, 1992, and a full phaseout by the end of the year. Kazuo Shima's fears had been realized. In my view, Japan agreed to driftnet negotiations—aware that such negotiations could lead to the end of driftnet fishing on the high seas—because of their broader interest in avoiding a significant deterioration in U.S.-Japanese relations, particularly the fisheries relationship.

The understanding that we entered into with Japan indeed confirmed the destructive nature of driftnet fleets and led to the banning of driftnet fishing on the high seas. Although some instances of driftnet fishing still occur, both illegally on the high seas and within the 200-mile EEZs of some countries, untold numbers of fish, seabirds, and marine mammals have been spared from dying in driftnets.

Succeeding against the Odds

The breakthrough in this negotiation came in the final meeting in Tokyo when the fisheries scientists on our delegations put together an agreement on an observer program that they agreed would yield statistically reliable data on the bycatch of the Japanese squid driftnet fleet. Once those data had been obtained, it was clear to me that—assuming that they confirmed our suppositions and anecdotal reports regarding the damage being done to the marine ecology—the end would be in sight for high-seas driftnet fishing. It was a significant breakthrough that we had gotten for the first time agreement to an observer program on a nonsalmon Japanese fishing fleet in international waters

The other elements of the agreement (such as position-finding transponders), while important, were less central to what we were trying to accomplish, and some compromises in the timing of their implementation were more acceptable. A negotiator will rarely get everything that he is seeking, and it is important to prioritize and concentrate on achieving the most critical goals.

Because Japan would not agree to everything we wanted in 1989, it was necessary to have its firm commitment to continue to cooperate with us and agree to expanded programs in the years that followed. This emphasis on a continuing process is a critical part of negotiations on most global environmental issues. Such negotiations generally involve matters that must be managed cooperatively over extended periods of time and need to be regularly revisited as scientific knowledge advances.

Another lesson of this negotiation, which is a common thread in most negotiations, is the importance of engaging and listening to those whose interests will be affected. I began my job as chief negotiator with angry, frustrated, and distrustful constituencies among environmentalists and fisheries interests, particularly those in Alaska. Including them in the process of developing our negotiating strategy—especially during my two trips to Juneau— was extremely helpful. Without their understanding and trust and their participation, I would not have had enough support to counteract congressional skepticism and resistance, and certification of Japan under the Driftnet Act could not have been avoided. In sum, it is essential for a negotiator to engage with all of the stakeholders, including those who are angry and may be opposed, at least initially, to seeking an agreement or to making any compromises in order to achieve one.

We had to persevere even when progress came at a painfully slow pace, given the time pressures imposed by the provisions of the Driftnet Act, because the cost of failure would be so high and the benefits of an agreement so great. As the U.S. ambassador to Japan, Michael Armacost, noted, the agreement would have far-reaching implications: "It, and the similar agreements with other driftnet fishing nations that will doubtless be modeled on it, can be seen as the cornerstone of effective, multilateral management of high seas resources."[9]

Senior State Department officials involved in managing our international economic relations expressed relief and satisfaction that the negotiations with Japan had been successfully concluded. Under Secretary for Economic Affairs Richard McCormack said in a letter to me, dated June 21, that we now had "an opportunity to avoid a damaging confrontation with Japan and developed an approach for addressing our driftnet concerns in a positive spirit of cooperation that best served our interest."

I believe that not only our interest but also Japan's were served by this agreement. Many of those on the Japanese side surely realized that the indiscriminate and destructive nature of driftnet fishing would ultimately be confirmed and that the days of high-seas driftnet fleets were numbered. It was not in Japan's interest to become increasingly isolated in world opinion as a result of well-founded criticism from environmentalists.

The negotiation of the driftnet agreement allowed Japan to respond to the results of a scientifically sound, international observer program in which Japan took part. The data that it collected gave Japan an opportunity to move away more gracefully from a discredited fishing technique. The findings of the observers were helpful to Japan in taking the unavoidable, but politically difficult step of phasing out its driftnet fishery. Thus, I suspect that my Japanese counterparts would agree, in retrospect, that the successful completion of our negotiation benefited all concerned.

chapter 3

Acid Rains on Canadian-U.S. Relations

In summer 1978, as the newly assigned head of Canadian affairs in the State Department, I learned about the problem of acid rain. This was to become a principal issue in U.S. relations with Canada, a problem with which I would be deeply involved over the following 13 years. Rarely does a Foreign Service Officer, who moves frequently from assignment to assignment, have the opportunity to be engaged in a complex issue in foreign relations over such an extended period.

My initial tutor on the subject, George Rejhon, was a dynamic and committed environment officer at the Canadian embassy. Acid rain—more properly termed "acid precipitation," because it includes acidified rain, snow, and fog—had become a major problem in Canada in the late 1970s. Hundreds of lakes, mostly in Ontario, had been identified as acidified to the point that they could no longer sustain aquatic life, and thousands more were considered threatened and vulnerable. Concerns were also raised about the possible health effects of heavy metals that were being leached from the soil as a result of acid precipitation and finding their way into the food chain.

Professor Harold Harvey of the University of Toronto was among the pioneers in acid rain research. In the mid-1960s, he observed that some lakes had become extremely acidified and identified this as the cause of disappearing fish stocks. Although acidified lakes appeared clean and crystal clear, this was not a sign of health: they were devoid of life.

Harvey and other involved scientists assumed that sulfur dioxide was the primary cause of the acidification and assumed that the huge International Nickel Company (INCO) smelter in Sudbury, Ontario, was the culprit. The scientists soon determined, however, that not enough sulfur dioxide was being emitted from INCO and other Ontario sources to account for what was happening. The Canadian scientists concluded that sulfur dioxide was being carried in the atmosphere for much greater distances than had been realized and that the acid rain problem was a transboundary issue, involving the United States as well as Canada.

For most of the following decade, acid rain remained a concern largely confined to scientific circles. By the latter half of the 1970s, however, Canadian media were giving broad coverage to the acid rain story, triggering an alarmed public reaction in Canada. Rejhon brought this message home to me: he said that Canada had determined that a large portion—perhaps as much as 50 percent—of the emissions of sulfur dioxide affecting Canada came from the United States through the atmosphere.

Ironically, to help deal with the local health effects of sulfur dioxide deposition, a number of smelters and coal-burning power plants in Canada and the United States had built extremely tall smokestacks to disperse their emissions. This had the unintended effect of contributing to the long-range transport of sulfur dioxide.

Faltering First Steps

The Canadian-U.S. relationship is so broad and deep that there are always some misunderstandings and difficult problems in play, some of which can seem intractable. Nonetheless, when Canada and the United States have a problem, they generally address it amicably and cooperate in trying to find a solution. A landmark in that regard, with respect to the environment, was the 1909

Boundary Waters Treaty, in which each country agreed not to pollute boundary waters to the injury of health or property in the other country. The treaty established the International Joint Commission (IJC), which is still active and has become a world-renowned mechanism for helping bordering countries manage boundary water issues. At a 1979 meeting in Detroit, the IJC took note of the acid rain problem and expressed its concern about the precursors of acid precipitation.

Cooperation between Canada and the United States on the issue of acid rain began in October 1978, when the two countries established the Bilateral Research Consultation Group, cochaired by the Canadian Department of External Affairs and the U.S. State Department. Its mandate was to coordinate research and develop a scientific database on acid rain. A year later, it reported that large areas of North America were vulnerable to acid rain, noting decreases in the number and diversity of fish in the lakes of northeastern Canada and evidence that suggested damage to forests and agriculture.

In November 1978, U.S. Secretary of State Cyrus Vance and his Canadian counterpart, Secretary of State for External Affairs Donald Jamieson, jointly announced the beginning of a series of informal discussions between Canada and the United States dealing with acid rain. As a result of those talks, Canada and the United States issued a joint statement in July 1979 that cited their shared concern over the problem and their determination to deal with it consistent with their long tradition of working together on environmental matters.

Canada welcomed this joint statement, but as no more than a tepid first step. Canada pressed the United States to move promptly to negotiate an air quality agreement that would result in reductions in the transboundary flows of sulfur dioxide in both directions. In response, the United States agreed to develop a joint memorandum of intent, stating that both countries intended to negotiate a bilateral agreement dealing with acid rain and to vigor-ously enforce existing air pollution legislation. This memorandum of intent, signed on August 5, 1980, established work groups to study the scientific and technical aspects of acid rain.

In the last months of the Carter administration, Congress established by law the National Acid Precipitation Assessment Program (NAPAP) and charged it with conducting scientific, technological, and economic analyses of the causes and effects of acid deposition. NAPAP was expected to take 10 years to complete its work, using an anticipated budget of $500 million. The process of addressing the acid rain problem was moving at an irritatingly slow pace from Canada's perspective, because it was suffering substantial damage to its lakes.

In summer 1980, I began a three-year posting as deputy chief of mission at the U.S. embassy in Ottawa. Pending the appointment of a new ambassador, I became chargé d'affaires when Kenneth Curtis, the ambassador appointed by President Carter, departed Canada on President Reagan's inauguration day, January 20, 1981. When President Reagan arrived in Ottawa in March 1981 for his first foreign trip as president, I accompanied him throughout his daylong visit. He was perplexed when hundreds of Canadian protestors greeted him with signs and chants of "Acid Rain, Go Home." It was apparently not an issue on which he had focused much attention.

In June 1981, Canada and the United States began talks aimed at concluding a bilateral agreement on transboundary air pollution. They did not go well. It soon became apparent that the United States still did not share Canada's sense of urgency. At the final session in this series of Canadian-U.S. talks on February 23, 1982, the United States rejected a Canadian proposal to reduce acid deposition in vulnerable areas to 20 kilograms per hectare per year (about half of 1980 levels).

The United States took the position that such specific reduction commitments—insisted on by Canada—were premature. The U.S. delegation was headed by Thomas Niles, a deputy assistant secretary of state in the Bureau of European and Canadian Affairs, who several years later was appointed U.S. ambassador to Canada. The U.S. side concluded that there was no way to bridge the differences, so this attempt to pursue negotiations on an air quality agreement ended.

Elements of an Impasse

Several reasons explain why Canada and the United States could not reach an agreement: The principal pollutant involved, sulfur dioxide, was produced in much greater quantity in the United States than in Canada, and the prevailing winds were such that more sulfur dioxide emissions were transported from the United States to Canada than in the other direction. Further, because of the Canadian Shield, a great slice of rock lying near the surface of much of central and eastern Canada, the capacity of Canadian soils to act as a buffer against acidification was far less than in the United States.

At the same time, the steps necessary to address the acid rain problem would be much more expensive and socially disruptive in the United States. Canada could achieve its necessary reductions in sulfur dioxide simply by cutting back on emissions from a handful of major sources, such as the Ontario metal smelters in Sudbury and Falconbridge. In the United States, the primary sources of sulfur dioxide emissions were numerous aging, coal-burning power plants spread across many states. Sharply reducing those emissions would be costly, involving the retrofitting of existing plants with expensive stack scrubbers for removing sulfur dioxide. This would lead to increases in the price of electricity in the industrial heartland of the United States, where many of the sulfur dioxide–emitting plants were located.

Sulfur dioxide emissions in the United States were actually decreasing, primarily as a result of the sulfur dioxide–reducing technologies required in new power plants under the 1963 Clean Air Act, subsequently amended several times. One provision of the 1970 amendments required that newly built power plants use the best available technologies to achieve reductions in sulfur dioxide emissions.[1] Increased use of lower sulfur coal and other cleaner fuels further contributed to those reductions. As a result, U.S. sulfur dioxide emissions dropped from a peak of 28 million metric tons in 1972 to an estimated 21 million metric tons in 1984.

NAPAP's initial progress report, issued in January 1981, stated that only a handful of U.S. lakes were suffering from acidification

and that at this stage NAPAP was uncertain about the vulner-
ability of other U.S. lakes to future acidification. NAPAP did find
damage to buildings from acid rain, as well as possible damage to
forest cover at upper altitudes. In addition, there was evidence of
significant visibility degradation as a result of sulfur dioxide emissions in the atmosphere. Although not nearly so alarming as the
situation in Canada, these interim NAPAP findings were troubling
enough to raise the U.S. level of concern, particularly in New York
and the New England states, which—like Canada—were in the
path of sulfur dioxide emissions originating in the U.S. Midwest.

Political considerations on the U.S. side were an additional
complication. Strip mining in the western states produced a
grade of coal that generally had lower sulfur content than the
coal produced in the mines of certain eastern states, particularly
West Virginia. Any program that encouraged more use of lower
sulfur coal would, therefore, economically disadvantage the
eastern coal-mining states, and resistance could be expected from
their representatives in Congress, including the powerful Senator
Robert Byrd (West Virginia).

Given all those factors, it was clear to me that the United States
was not prepared to embark on a costly program to achieve further
reductions in emissions of acid rain precursors, particularly sulfur
dioxide, until we had (1) fully understood the problem of acid rain
and what steps would be effective in countering it and (2) reached
a consensus within the United States on how the domestic financial, social, and political costs of dealing with it would be shared.
Thus, an extended period of increasing tension between Canada
and the United States over this difficult issue ensued.

During the 1980s, acid rain continued to be a dominant
problem in Canadian-U.S. relations. Canadian leaders, including
Prime Minister Brian Mulroney, often referred to the U.S. response
on acid rain as the "litmus test" for our relationship. The U.S.
side tried to find ways of working cooperatively with Canada to
share research and advance our understanding of the acid rain
issue. Canada, however, viewed our efforts as wholly inadequate
and believed that President Reagan did not place a high priority
on resolving the acid rain problem. The president consistently

stopped short of making specific commitments to reduce levels of the atmospheric pollutants that caused acid rain. As frustration levels rose, Canada began handing out literature about acid rain at the Canadian-U.S. border.

During these years, Canada made progress in dealing with acid rain domestically. On March 6, 1985, just a week and a half before a scheduled meeting with President Reagan, Prime Minister Mulroney announced a Canadian acid rain control program that would cut sulfur dioxide emissions in the seven easternmost provinces by 50 percent and halve the amount of acid rain that Canada exported to the United States.

Reagan Reengages on Acid Rain

In what became known as the "Shamrock Summit," Reagan met with Mulroney in Quebec City on St. Patrick's Day, March 17, 1985. Acid rain was prominent on the agenda of the two ethnically Irish leaders. They each appointed a personal special envoy to examine the acid rain issue and report back to them before their next summit meeting, scheduled for spring 1986. The two special envoys, former Ontario Premier William Davis and former U.S. Transportation Secretary Drew Lewis, were to work together to produce a joint report on this contentious environmental issue.

The joint Davis-Lewis report, issued in January 1986, stated clearly that acid rain was a serious transboundary issue that needed to be addressed by both countries. In addition to the usual calls for cooperation in acid precipitation research and monitoring, it also recommended a $5 billion program, funded half by the U.S. government and half by U.S. industry, for building pilot projects to prove the viability of clean coal technologies. (The U.S. Department of Energy had already been conducting research to identify such clean coal technologies.[2]) The report also called for setting up an advisory body to help the secretary of energy choose the pilot projects to be pursued; a Canadian government official would be a member of this U.S. advisory body.

When they met in Washington in March 1986, Reagan and Mulroney fully endorsed the joint report of the special envoys and agreed to implement its recommendations. At their next meeting, in Ottawa in April 1987, the two leaders agreed to consider a Canadian proposal for an accord on acid rain. In May, Canada submitted such a proposal, which included as a central element the establishment by the United States of specific targets and time-tables for the reduction of sulfur dioxide emissions.

By this time, I had moved on to be principal deputy assistant secretary of state for the Bureau of Oceans and International Environmental and Scientific Affairs. Assistant Secretary John Negroponte had picked me for the job in part because of my experience in working on Canadian matters, and he assigned the acid rain issue to me. I took on that task, aware that the United States was not in a position to make a commitment to Canada concerning sulfur dioxide reductions until the U.S. Congress had acted on this issue.

I believed that, even though the United States could not yet make specific commitments on sulfur dioxide reductions, it was in the interest of both countries to negotiate an agreement with commitments on joint monitoring, research, and consultations, plus a commitment to the future development of agreed goals for reduced sulfur dioxide emissions.

In spring 1988, Secretary of State George Shultz proposed such an agreement. The Canadians declined, however, taking the position that they could not enter into any agreement on acid rain that did not include specific goals and timetables for sulfur dioxide reductions. They preferred to wait until after the upcoming U.S. presidential election and work with the incoming administration on this issue. Their dealings with the Reagan administration had convinced them that a successor administration, whether Republican or Democratic, would view the acid rain problem with more urgency and would make a better partner in seeking an agreement to resolve it.

Targets and Timetables

George H. W. Bush, who succeeded Reagan as president, had

long been viewed by Canada as more sympathetic to its acid rain concerns. In February 1989, shortly after his inauguration, President Bush met in Ottawa with Prime Minister Mulroney. At that meeting, Bush announced that negotiations with Canada on a bilateral accord addressing the acid rain problem could begin as soon as he submitted to Congress a comprehensive proposal for reauthorizing the Clean Air Act. That proposal, submitted to Congress in July 1989, included specific reductions in sulfur dioxide and nitrogen oxides to be achieved on a specified timetable.

The proposed reduction in sulfur dioxide emissions, 10 million tons by 2000, was set at a level that we knew was adequate to meet Canada's requirements. Politically, the concerns of West Virginia and other eastern coal-mining states about disadvantaging their high-sulfur coal producers were being offset by growing apprehension in the northeastern states that their environment was threatened by acid rain. The outlook for the legislation in Congress was promising.

At Assistant Secretary Negroponte's request, I headed the U.S. team for the negotiation with Canada. My role was reinforced when I received a letter from President Bush, dated March 22, 1990, according me the rank of ambassador in my capacity as special negotiator for acid rain talks with Canada. The ambassadorial designation not only reflected the importance the president placed on the negotiations but also was helpful because my Canadian counterpart, Michael Phillips, assistant deputy minister in charge of U.S. relations, held a more senior position in the Canadian Department of External Affairs than I did at the U.S. State Department.

The first problem was one of timing. Although Canada was expecting a prompt start to the negotiations, I realized that if talks on emissions targets and timetables began before Congress acted on President Bush's proposal to amend the Clean Air Act, the State Department could be accused of being presumptuous with regard to legislative prerogatives. I knew that there was significant sensitivity on the Hill (for example, on the part of Representative John Dingell of Michigan, who felt that we were allowing Canada to have undue influence over U.S. domestic decisions on environmental issues). Also, I needed time to thoroughly brief concerned congressional staffers on our proposed negotiating strategy and listen to their views before engaging in substantive negotiations with the Canadians.

To deal with this problem, we obtained Canada's understanding that we would begin our acid rain talks as a discussion about the proposed structure of an acid rain agreement and the provisions that we would want it to contain. We agreed that we would not begin negotiations on the substance of the agreement until the U.S. Congress voted on the Clean Air Act reauthorization. This not only avoided antagonizing Congress but also provided a useful period during which the Canadian and U.S. negotiating teams could lay the groundwork for the negotiation. I assured concerned congressional staffers that these preliminary talks with Canada would not result in any premature U.S. commitments.

To begin our discussion, each side prepared an "elements of an agreement" paper that laid out what each country wanted to have in the accord. During the talks that followed, in Washington and Ottawa, we confirmed our intention to make the accord a broad air quality agreement that provided a strong institutional mechanism for dealing with not only the acid rain problem but all future transboundary air quality issues. Both sides were determined that any future issue involving the cross-border transport of air pollutants be better and more expeditiously handled than was the acid rain dispute.

We held several rounds of these preliminary talks with the Canadians until the U.S. Congress acted. Comparable bills on the Clean Air Act reauthorization were voted out of the Senate on April 3, 1990, and the House of Representatives on May 23, 1990. They contained virtually identical provisions on reduction goals and timetables for sulfur dioxide and nitrogen oxides, consistent with the administration's request.

At the G-7 economic summit meeting[3] held in Houston in July 1990, Bush and Mulroney announced their agreement to start negotiations to address acid rain and other air pollution concerns. On July 16, 1990, U.S. EPA Administrator William Reilly and Canadian Environment Minister Robert de Cotret met to follow up on their leaders' Houston announcement. They issued a joint statement declaring that negotiations would begin in Ottawa on August 28, 1990, on a Canada-U.S. air quality accord that would establish a framework for managing a comprehensive range of transboundary pollutants.[4] They cited the overall purpose of the accord as being to "provide Canada and the U.S. with a practical and effective instrument to deal with shared problems of transboundary air pollutants." Specifically, their statement said that the accord would do the following:

> Commit both countries, with the objective of reducing damage caused by transboundary flows of emissions, to develop and implement measures to control emissions of airborne pollutants, and to establish specific goals and schedules for reductions of sulphur dioxide and other agreed upon air pollutants.[5]

The Reilly–de Cotret statement noted several other things that the accord would do: (1) require consideration of the transboundary impact of domestic activities and provide for prior notification, consultation, and consideration of mitigating measures; (2) require the development of coordinated research and monitoring programs; and (3) establish a means for impartial oversight and dispute settlement. Thus, we were to begin formal negotiations working from a clear directive on what we were expected to achieve.

The statement named me to head the negotiation as special negotiator, with Eileen Claussen, director of EPA's Office of Air and Radiation, as the alternate head of the U.S. negotiating team. The Canadian side was to be led by Phillips. Dr. Robert Slater, an assistant deputy minister in Environment Canada—the Canadian counterpart to EPA—was designated as Canada's conegotiator.

Negotiations at Last

I had long been concerned about the inflammatory rhetoric on acid rain that had been crossing the border over the years. As a first order of business, I sought and obtained the agreement of my Canadian counterparts to conduct these negotiations with traditional diplomatic restraint and to take steps to prevent leaks aimed at obtaining public support for our respective positions while they were under negotiation. We agreed that at the end of each negotiating session, we would issue a joint press statement and otherwise avoid making statements to the media about the state of the negotiations.

In the first two rounds of negotiations, we made good progress in merging our two proposed agreement texts, and we readily confirmed a couple of basic points: the agreement would establish a process for addressing air quality issues in general, and it would contain binding commitments for reductions in emissions of acid rain precursors, particularly sulfur dioxide.

Two issues emerged, however, on which we differed sharply:

(1) The United States held that, with regard to specific objectives, the commitment must be stated in terms of domestic emissions reductions as contained in the Clean Air Act amendments; Canada pressed for an additional standard that would call for specific reductions in transboundary flows of the pollutants that caused acid rain.

(2) The U.S. side argued that each party should be able to make amendments to its domestic programs without the concurrence of the other party; Canada insisted on a concurrence requirement for such amendments, arguing that it would be impossible to justify an agreement under which the U.S. obligation could be altered unilaterally.

At the third round of negotiations, we made substantial further progress. The Canadians agreed that there was merit to our argument that transboundary flows of pollutants were too uncertain and difficult to measure to make them a standard for commitments under the agreement. They accepted that the standard for such commitments would be domestic emissions reductions.

The U.S. side, in turn, accepted the Canadian position that the annex to the accord, which contained the specific commitments to reductions in emissions of acid rain precursors, could be amended only by mutual consent. We insisted, however, that this made it necessary for them to address and respond more fully to our concerns about specific aspects of their program. For example, we considered it necessary that they include a commitment, as we did in the Clean Air Act amendments, to reduce emissions of nitrogen oxides, which are implicated with sulfur dioxide as a contributing cause of acid rain. Also, we had enacted a national cap on emissions of the acid rain precursors—sulfur dioxide and nitrogen oxides—that would come into force once the specified emissions reductions had been achieved, and we argued that it was necessary for Canada to do the same.

Although the Canadian side acknowledged that our demands for strengthening the Canadian domestic program were soundly based, they were reluctant to respond immediately because, under their federal system, they felt a need to obtain the agreement of their provinces before undertaking such additional obligations. They said that they would be discussing the issues that we raised in a meeting of the federal government with the provincial governments scheduled for November 28–29, 1990. We agreed to have another negotiating session in Washington in December, at which the Canadians would be prepared to address our concerns.

Meanwhile, on November 15, 1990, the president signed into law the Clean Air Act Amendments of 1990.

The Air Quality Accord

The burden had shifted to the Canadians. They would have to improve their acid rain program to make it comparable to the more stringent U.S. program under the reauthorization of the Clean Air Act and its amendments. That was all that stood between us and the successful completion of the negotiation.

When the Canadians came to Washington in December, they were prepared to make the changes that we had requested. Phillips and I then initialed each page of the negotiating draft, indicating that the negotiators for Canada and the United States had reached agreement and had in hand an accord that they were ready to recommend to their respective governments for signature.

The commitments in the accord—known as the Canada-U.S. Air Quality Agreement—that related to acid rain were summarized as follows in an article that I wrote with Susan Biniaz, who represented the State Department's legal adviser on my delegation:

> In an attempt to put to rest the acid rain dispute, the Agreement specifically focuses on the principal acid rain precursors. To this end, it contains in an annex concrete objectives for SO_2 and NO_x emissions reductions or limitations which each country is to achieve. These objectives are framed as international legal commitments. For example, with respect to SO_2 emissions, the United States will reduce annual emissions by approximately ten million tons from 1980 levels by the year 2000, and will achieve a permanent national emissions cap of 8.95 million tons for electric utilities by the year 2010. Canada, similarly, will reduce emissions in the seven easternmost provinces to 2.3 million tons per year by 1994, achieve a cap in those provinces at 2.3 million tons per year from 1995 through 2000, and achieve a permanent national emissions cap of 3.2 million tons per year by the year 2000.[6]

The agreement also calls for notification and consultation on proposed actions that, if carried out, would be likely to cause significant transboundary air pollution. It commits the parties to take appropriate measures to avoid or mitigate the risks posed by such actions. Further, it calls on the parties to coordinate scientific and technical activities. In the words of the agreement, such cooperation is intended to "improve their understanding of transboundary air pollution concerns and to increase their capability to control such pollution."

The accord institutionalizes a strong monitoring and oversight function through the establishment of a joint Air Quality Committee, chaired at the assistant secretary level in the U.S. State Department and the Canadian Department of External Affairs. This committee is charged with assisting in the agreement's implementation and preparing regular progress reports at least every two years. The agreement also contains strong settlement provisions for dealing with any disputes that might arise under the accord.

The Air Quality Agreement gives the IJC a significant role: to invite comments from the public on the reports of the Air Quality Committee, hold public hearings on them when appropriate, and submit a report to the parties to the accord on the views of the public.

Thus, Canada and the United States went well beyond what was required to deal with the acid rain problem and elected to take the opportunity to create a broad legal and institutional framework for addressing all transboundary air pollution issues. The accord established the machinery needed to ensure not only that the acid rain issue was successfully addressed but also that future air quality problems would be identified early and handled from the beginning in a more systematic and cooperative mode.

I joined President Bush on Air Force One on March 13, 1991, for the flight to Ottawa, where he and Prime Minister Mulroney signed the Canada-U.S. Air Quality Agreement. At the signing ceremony, Bush graciously recognized the work of the negotiating teams on both sides.

Acid Test of Canadian-U.S. Relations

Perhaps more than with any other country, the United States has made the calculation that given the vast array of interrelations between the two countries, a good and close working relationship with Canada is critically important to us. Therefore, the United States conducts its dealings with Canada accordingly. The relationship has its ups and downs and is sometimes burdened with long-standing, emotionally charged disputes. However, both countries consistently work to deal with issues on their merits and, when a problem cannot be quickly resolved, to find a way to manage it that minimizes contentiousness until a solution can be found. The difficult and long-running acid rain dispute strained, but did not break, the mold of this cooperative relationship.

One key to the ability of Canada and the United States to ultimately resolve their differences on acid rain was that, over a period of many years, we kept finding ways to stay engaged. When we were not ready to have meaningful negotiations, we set up consultative groups and worked through special envoys. Even in the final stages, our engagement in months of prenegotiation talks kept us from losing momentum as we waited for Congress to complete its work on the Clean Air Act Amendments of 1990.

The actual negotiation of the Air Quality Agreement went quickly and smoothly because the foundation for it had been so well prepared. We did not try to proceed with the negotiations before the acid rain issues had been resolved domestically in the United States, which would have been fruitless. We began the negotiations only when we had the amendments to the Clean Air Act in hand so that both sides knew the extent to which we could commit to reductions in emissions of acid rain precursors. Moreover, our restraint in this regard gave me and my negotiating team time to consult adequately with Congress. This ensured that the legislative branch of government fully understood and accepted what we were seeking to accomplish with the agreement.

The direct and substantial involvement of the leaders in both countries was critical to keeping us on track to resolution. From the Shamrock Summit in 1985 until the signing of the Air Quality Agreement in 1991, the president of the United States and the prime minister of Canada met annually, with acid rain at the top of their agenda. Less than a month after his inauguration in January 1989, Bush met with Mulroney and firmly committed to amending the Clean Air Act and obtaining the authority needed to negotiate with Canada on reducing emissions of acid rain precursors. It helped me considerably in bringing those negotiations to a successful conclusion when Bush subsequently buttressed my authority by naming me a special negotiator with the rank of ambassador.

It was also helpful that the United States, with EPA taking the lead, was able to substantially reduce the cost—and related increases in electric power rates—of implementing its commitments under the Air Quality Agreement through an innovative system that allowed emitting sources to trade in emissions permits. With this cap-and-trade mechanism, power plants that were the most cost-efficient in making reductions in sulfur dioxide emissions could reduce emissions beyond their own requirements and then sell their additional emissions-reducing capacity to other power plants, allowing those plants to avoid making more costly reductions. In this way, any given amount of sulfur dioxide emissions reduction could be achieved at the lowest total cost.

The Air Quality Agreement has functioned as intended and become another success story in Canadian-U.S. relations. The 15-year progress report (2006) prepared by the joint Air Quality Committee established under the agreement confirmed that the two countries were continuing to honor all their commitments and are continuing to meet to consider the adequacy of the steps that they have taken.[7] The goals for sulfur dioxide and nitrogen oxides emissions reductions have been exceeded in both countries. Canadian and U.S. surface waters have, in general, become significantly less acidified as a result. Some lakes, however, still have acid levels too high to support healthy populations of fish and other marine life, and more emissions reductions are planned by the two countries in further implementation of the agreement.

An ozone annex was added to the agreement in 2000 aimed at reducing ground-level concentrations of ozone, nitrogen oxides, and volatile organic compounds in border areas, and both countries are on track to meet the reduction targets contained in that annex. A new annex that would call for reductions in emissions of particulate matter is currently under consideration. Active public participation and input have been stimulated through meetings held by the IJC. The 15-year progress report sums up our experience as follows:

> This agreement has provided important opportunities for collaboration between Canada and the United States and has produced impressive results, not just in environmental improvements, but also in diplomacy and working relationships. Both countries rely on the Agreement as the mechanism to address air pollution issues and are committed to its continuing viability and relevance as new bilateral issues emerge. The Agreement's

flexibility provides opportunities to go beyond the challenges identified by the Acid Rain and Ozone annexes, and the Parties look forward to considering whether and how to address bilateral issues associated with particulate matter, mercury, and other pollutants.[8]

chapter 4

Caribou in the Oil Patch

The Porcupine caribou herd, which migrates between Canada and the United States, is the world's largest transboundary caribou herd, generally ranging between 120,000 and 180,000 head over the past 25 years. It is named for the Porcupine River, which flows through its habitat. Like migrating birds, the herd moves northward in the summer and southward in the winter.

Although the herd spends most of the year in the Canadian Yukon and Northwest territories, a critical portion of its annual cycle takes place in the 19-million-acre Arctic National Wildlife Refuge (ANWR), located in an isolated and sparsely populated portion of northeastern Alaska. It is on ANWR's coastal plain that the herd makes its summer calving grounds. The refuge provides highly nutritious grazing and serves as a place to find relief from predators and harassing hordes of insects. ANWR has also gained renown as the likely location of the largest untapped oil reserves in the United States.[1]

The herd has special importance to both Canada and the United States, in part because it serves as a source of sustenance for Native populations in both countries. The hunting of caribou in the Porcupine herd is particularly important for the Gwitchin people, who live in settlements throughout the habitat of the caribou, including in the south of ANWR. Without a healthy herd,

— *Carl Stoiber*

the Gwitchin would be unable to maintain their traditional way of life. In contrast, the Inupiat people who live in Kaktovik, a village located along the northern boundary of ANWR, rely primarily on whaling as a source of protein and would accept oil and gas development in ANWR that did not unduly interfere with their way of life.

Any disruption in either Alaska or Canada of the herd's precisely timed annual migration pattern could have disastrous effects on its well-being. For example, any action that delayed its arrival in the Alaskan calving grounds or disturbed its stay there could profoundly affect the herd's ability to reproduce. Thus, there is an obvious need for Canada and the United States to closely consult and coordinate on activities that might affect the herd or its habitat.

In Pursuit of a Treaty

In 1978, aware of the potential risks posed by uncoordinated actions, the U.S. Department of the Interior asked the Department of State for authority to negotiate a treaty with Canada that would provide for jointly managing the herd. The request for that authority was contained in a letter dated August 28 from David Hales, acting assistant secretary of the interior for fish and wildlife and parks, to Clyde McClelland, acting assistant secretary of state for the Bureau of Oceans and International Environmental and Scientific Affairs. Hales closed his letter to McClelland with an impassioned plea on behalf of the caribou:

> The plight of this magnificent migratory species demands that action be taken now or our nation's last remaining opportunity for its preservation may be lost forever. The Porcupine herd, by virtue of its calving grounds in Alaska and its wintering grounds in Canada, is precariously balanced on an international boundary that is significant to nations but not to migratory species. Today it faces increasingly stiff competition from the development of its heretofore isolated habitat. Presently, national and international attention is focused on this region and on these caribou. The opportunity for international cooperation may never be the same. I urge you to act expeditiously in order that this opportunity not be lost.

In response to the Department of the Interior's request, OES initiated the so-called Circular 175 procedure. This procedure seeks to confirm that the making of international agreements by the United States is carried out within legal limitations, with due consideration of an agreement's foreign policy implications and with appropriate involvement by the State Department. The typical Circular 175 request is a memorandum from a bureau or office in the State Department to a State official at the assistant secretary level or above, seeking authority to negotiate, conclude, amend, extend, or terminate an international agreement. It usually states the issue for decision, the factors involved, and a recommendation for action.

On October 2, 1979, Under Secretary of State for International Security Affairs Lucy Benson approved the Circular 175 request for authority to negotiate a treaty with Canada dealing with the conservation of caribou. The U.S. Fish and Wildlife Service of the Department of the Interior then began discussions with its Canadian counterpart.

The Canadian-U.S. talks were inconclusive. I was not involved in these talks, but I observed their progress—or rather lack of progress—from my positions as country director for Canada in the State Department and later, from 1980 to 1983, as deputy chief of mission at the U.S. embassy in Ottawa. There was underlying uneasiness in both Canada and the United States that a bilateral commission envisioned under the proposed treaty could preempt the legitimate roles of each of the two countries in managing the herd. Sporadic talks continued in the years that followed, but made no progress.

Renewed Negotiation Initiative

In August 1985, I began my assignment as principal deputy assistant secretary in OES. The assistant secretary for the bureau, John Negroponte, asked me to draw on my background in Canadian affairs to pay special attention to the many issues that involved Canada, especially in the environment and conservation area. I had long been frustrated by the inability of Canada and the United States to negotiate an agreement dealing with the management of transboundary caribou and decided to make the completion of an agreement a priority.

William Horn, assistant secretary of the interior for fish and wildlife and parks, reviewed with me the state of our talks with Canada about the Porcupine caribou. He agreed with my suggestion that I take over as the U.S. negotiator and see whether we could get the stalled negotiations moving forward. My first tasks were to identify the obstacles to an agreement and develop a negotiating strategy that could overcome them.

The primary problem concerned the establishment of an

independent bilateral commission with authority to manage the herd. This treaty-based commission would have operational management responsibility that went beyond what federal and local authorities in either country were apparently prepared to accept. The governments of Alaska and the Yukon and Northwest territories, as well as the two federal governments, all had responsibilities for management of the herd that they were not willing to relinquish to a binational commission.

The need as I saw it was to move away from the treaty approach and pursue an executive agreement, which would be less intrusive. Unlike the treaty that had been sought, an executive agreement would not affect the existing pattern of laws and regulations in each country. The agreement would have at its heart a mechanism for facilitating consultation and coordination between Canada and the United States on activities that would affect the herd. Like a treaty, an executive agreement is considered to be a commitment of the United States, not just the administration that negotiates it.

Rather than a commission with independent powers, this new approach would establish an advisory, binational board on which the relevant authorities in both countries and the principal users of the herd and its habitat would be represented. The board would be empowered to make recommendations to the two countries regarding the management of the herd, but those recommendations would not be mandatory. Also, the governments of Canada and the United States would agree to consult in advance regarding any activities that would significantly affect the caribou.

Moving from a treaty to an executive agreement required a new Circular 175 request for negotiating authority. This authority was granted on October 30, 1986, by Under Secretary of State for Coordinating Security Assistance Programs William Schneider. I promptly contacted John Noble, director general of the United States Relations Bureau in the Department of External Affairs in Canada. Noble enthusiastically agreed to proceed with the negotiation of an agreement on this new basis. He said that he would take over as leader of the Canadian negotiating team and join me in an effort to bring the negotiation to an early conclusion.

The question now was how to structure the negotiation. For nearly a decade, there had been ample discussion of the issues involved. The difficulty was the markedly different perspectives of stakeholders in the herd and its habitat. These stakeholders included governmental authorities, Native peoples, and private entities interested in exploiting resources in the herd's habitat, particularly in ANWR. If an agreement were to be concluded, compromises would have to be reached that were acceptable to all of these interest groups.

I concluded that the best approach would be to have a single negotiating session attended by all interested parties. The intent of such a meeting would be to create a draft agreement to which all the participants could commit and undertake to defend within their respective interest groups. Noble agreed with this approach. We realized that it would be an unwieldy meeting, but we saw no alternative that was more likely to produce an agreement.

The Seattle Meeting

John Noble and I decided to hold the negotiation at the Sheraton Hotel and Towers in Seattle on December 1–3, 1986. This location was chosen as a middle ground, reasonably convenient for all the parties involved, including the federal, state, and territorial officials. Also, all the participants would be living and working together, away from the distractions that inevitably arise in national capital cities. I viewed it as an optimal negotiating environment for what we would be trying to accomplish.

In putting together the U.S. delegation, I sought to have all the stakeholders represented. The Interior Department had several members on the delegation, ensuring participation not only by those in Interior concerned with wildlife issues but also by those responsible for regulating the exploration and use of natural resources on federal lands. There were also three representatives of Native peoples, including the Gwitchin, whose livelihood depended on the herd, and the Inupiat from Kaktovik village. Others on the delegation included a staffer from the office of

Senator Frank Murkowski (Alaska) and representatives from the Alaska Department of Fish and Game and the Alaska Oil and Gas Association. To bring on board a well-known and highly regarded conservationist, I invited Curtis (Buff) Bohlen of the World Wildlife Fund to join the delegation. (Several years later, Bohlen served as assistant secretary of state for OES.)

The U.S. delegation in Seattle had 18 members, plus several others attending as observers. Canada was represented by a similarly large and diverse negotiating team. In our opening statements, Noble and I both made clear that we were in Seattle to complete a draft of the agreement. We emphasized that all the affected interest groups were well represented, and the time had come to work out any necessary compromises and overcome any remaining obstacles to an agreement. We were prepared to work all day and into the evenings to do so. Further, we had made arrangements with the hotel to extend the meeting beyond the three days scheduled if more time were required to successfully complete the negotiation.

The meeting proceeded as Noble and I hoped it would. In the large plenary meetings, we were quickly able to identify the issues that needed to be resolved. The differences fell along predictable lines. Certain representatives of Native peoples, especially the Gwitchin, wanted maximum assurances that the caribou would be shielded from any activities in their habitat that might undermine the herd's well-being. Others, including the Kaktovik Inupiat, representatives of the oil and gas industry, and the state of Alaska, had concerns about protecting other potential uses of the habitat. The differences were as great among members of the U.S. delegation as they were between the delegations of the two countries.

As planned, there were enough representatives of the interest groups that they could caucus and contact their home bases to determine how far they could go in agreeing to compromises. Noble and I met separately with interest groups from our respective delegations to encourage them to find workable solutions to the problems that arose in the negotiation.

We were able to reach agreement readily on several points.

The agreement would include a commitment by Canada and the United States to consult with each other before taking any action that could have a significant effect on the Porcupine caribou or their habitat. There would be a ban on the commercial sale of meat obtained from the herd. As a central feature of the agreement, an international board would be established that would be charged with making recommendations to the two countries about the management of the herd.

Much of our time was spent dealing with the issue of how this board would be constituted and how it would function. We reached agreement that it would consist of two national sections, each with four members to be appointed by the respective countries. The number was significant because it was enough to give both sides confidence that the interests of all the various entities involved—including federal, state, and provincial governments, Native peoples, and the private sector—could be adequately represented.

The final issues to resolve were how the board would decide to make recommendations to the governments of Canada and the United States and what would be the status of those recommendations. The compromise reached on the status of the recommendations was that they would not be mandatory, but that the two countries would commit to considering them and responding to them in writing.

The board's decisionmaking formula presented the most difficult problem. The principle of consensus decisionmaking would be a formula for stalemate, given the diverse interests represented on the board. A majority vote approach raised the specter of alliances between elements in the two national sections that could lead to unacceptable results. For example, the four Canadian members could combine with just one from the U.S. side, thus forming a majority opposed by three of the four U.S. board members.

To deal with this last barrier, Noble and I proposed that a decision by the board to submit a recommendation to the two countries would require support of a majority of both the Canadian and the U.S. members of the board. Thus, every board member would be assured that no recommendation with which he or she disagreed would go forward unless it was supported by three of the four members of the national section. Also, this approach would not allow any one member from either country to block a recommendation, as would consensus decisionmaking. This innovative decisionmaking procedure proved acceptable to all the interests represented at the meeting and cleared the way to prepare an agreed negotiating text. On December 3, 1986, Noble and I initialed a draft of the "Agreement between the Government of the United States and the Government of Canada on the Conservation of the Porcupine Caribou Herd." By doing so, we committed ourselves to recommend its signature to our respective governments.

ANWR Oil Issues

When I returned to Washington, I discovered that there was continuing uneasiness about the effect that an agreement might have on decisions regarding the development of oil reserves in ANWR. Don Perlman, an assistant to Interior Secretary Donald Hodel, appeared especially concerned that the agreement would limit U.S. flexibility in making those decisions.

Senator Murkowski also expressed some misgivings about the agreement's potential effect on the development of oil resources in ANWR. The governor of Alaska, Steve Cowper, however, was supportive and recommended that the draft agreement be formalized and signed by both countries.

Within days of the initialing of the agreement, the Department of the Interior released a draft report proposing that a part of ANWR be opened for oil exploration and development. The report asserted that as much as 9.2 billion barrels of oil might lie beneath ANWR and argued that the reserves in this petroleum "superfield" were urgently needed. The Canadian government expressed both its concern that oil development in ANWR could have unacceptable consequences for the Porcupine caribou and its disappointment that it had not been consulted before the draft report was released. I also was caught off guard by the release of the report.

In January and February 1987, I received letters from Mark Schneider of the Standard Oil Company expressing concern about the Porcupine caribou herd agreement and the effect that it could have on oil development in ANWR. I responded to him in a letter dated March 5, 1987, in which I argued the merits of the agreement:

> The Porcupine Caribou Herd agreement provides a needed means for contributing to our ability to coordinate the management of an important trans-boundary resource in a rational way. If it makes sense to have such an agreement, and I believe it does, then it makes sense to do so quite apart from whatever other exchanges on land use in the area are taking place. In fact, the better argument based on the situation described in your letter is that now more than ever there is a need for a disciplined and structured mechanism for addressing these questions bilaterally, such as that provided for in the draft PCH [Porcupine caribou herd] agreement.

The language in the draft agreement made clear that its commitments were subject to domestic laws and regulations in Canada and the United States. The Department of the Interior, however, now insisted on inserting an additional reference to "national policies" in the two countries, believing that this would make the agreement less of a constraint on U.S. consideration of oil development in ANWR.

Canada was understandably wary of the change being proposed by the Interior Department. Noble, my negotiating counterpart, said Canada would be prepared to accept the change, but only if I would say in a letter to him that the change was not intended to undermine the commitments undertaken elsewhere in the agreement. The Interior Department countered that my letter to Noble could say that the reference to national policies was not intended "to vitiate the objectives of the agreement." This weaker proposed language was not acceptable to the Canadian side.

Disagreement on this final point seemed intractable. However, on the assumption that we would ultimately be able to resolve this problem in a way that would be satisfactory to the United

States, Interior Secretary Donald Hodel said that he would travel to Ottawa on July 17, 1987, to join Canadian Minister of Environment Tom McMillan in signing the agreement. As that date approached, I became increasingly concerned that we were not succeeding in breaking this impasse.

A Photo Finish in Ottawa

I was visiting our embassy in Ottawa on July 16 with this issue still unresolved. I argued that the Canadian proposal was a reasonable one and that we should agree to it. Given what I knew of his position, I was convinced that Perlman was advising the secretary not to sign the agreement unless Canada accepted our additional language in the agreement, together with Interior's preferred reference to not vitiating the objectives of the agreement, which would be contained in a letter from me to Noble. I saw no prospect that Canada would agree to those terms.

Fearing the worst, I prepared a draft telegram to be sent to the State Department in Washington if Secretary Hodel decided not to come to Ottawa to sign the agreement the following day. The telegram laid out my position and read in part as follows:

> AS THE NEGOTIATOR OF THE PCH [PORCUPINE CARIBOU HERD] AGREEMENT, I AM DEEPLY CONCERNED THAT OUR CURRENT POSITION ON THE ADDITION OF A REFERENCE TO NATIONAL POLICIES TO THE INITIALED DRAFT THREATENS TO BLOCK THE SCHEDULED SIGNING OF THE AGREEMENT ON FRIDAY IN OTTAWA.
>
> I WOULD MAKE SEVERAL POINTS:
>
> —THE ADDITION OF "NATIONAL POLICIES" TO THE INITIALED TEXT IS NOT NECESSARY. A REFERENCE TO DOMESTIC LAWS AND REGULATIONS IN AN INTERNATIONAL AGREEMENT IS SUFFICIENTLY BROAD TO INCLUDE EXECUTIVE ORDERS OR OTHER OFFICIAL U.S. POLICY STATEMENTS MADE PURSUANT TO LAW.

—THE CANADIANS ARE PREPARED TO ACCEPT THE "NATIONAL POLICY" REFERENCE AS LONG AS WE STATE IN MY LETTER TO JOHN NOBLE WHAT SHOULD BE OBVIOUS, I.E., IT IS NOT OUR INTENT TO UNDERMINE THROUGH THAT REFERENCE OUR COMMITMENTS UNDER THE AGREEMENT.

—IF WE INSIST ON SUCH A REFERENCE WITHOUT SUCH A CAVEAT, THE CANADIANS VIEW THE AGREE-MENT AS ESSENTIALLY MEANINGLESS. IT WOULD THEN BE READ AS A COMMITMENT, FOR EXAMPLE, TO TAKE INTO ACCOUNT THE WELFARE OF THE HERD ONLY IF IT DOESN'T CONFLICT WITH SOME OTHER POLICY—CLEARLY A COMMITMENT NOT WORTH HAVING, AND CERTAINLY NOT WHAT I NEGOTIATED.

IF WE ALLOW THE AGREEMENT TO COLLAPSE ON THE BASIS OF OUR CURRENT POSITION, WE WILL BE SEEN AS HAVING CAUSED THAT RESULT BY INSISTING ON AN UNNEEDED CHANGE TO THE NEGOTIATED DRAFT WHILE REFUSING EVEN TO CONFIRM THAT IT IS NOT OUR INTEN-TION TO UNDERMINE THEREBY THE COMMITMENTS WE HAD UNDERTAKEN ELSEWHERE IN THE AGREEMENT. THE NEGATIVE REPERCUSSIONS FOR U.S./CANADA RELATIONS, AND I WOULD ARGUE FOR OUR CREDIBILITY IN INTERNA-TIONAL NEGOTIATIONS, WOULD BE SUBSTANTIAL.

I STRONGLY URGE THAT WE AGREE EITHER TO REMOVE THE "NATIONAL POLICY" REFERENCE OR TO INCLUDE A STATEMENT IN MY LETTER TO NOBLE THAT IT IS NOT OUR INTENTION THEREBY TO UNDERMINE THE COMMITMENTS UNDERTAKEN ELSEWHERE IN THE AGREEMENT.

Late that day, I received word that Secretary Hodel would indeed be coming to Ottawa the following morning prepared to sign the agreement on the understanding that my letter to Noble make clear, as Canada had proposed, that our addition of "national policies" to the agreement text was not intended to undermine other provisions of the agreement. Thus, I fortunately did not have to send my last-minute telegram seeking a reconsideration of the U.S. position.

The signing ceremony on July 17 went smoothly, and Secretary Hodel appeared well pleased by the warm reception that the agreement received.

The Keys to Success

The shift from a binational commission established by treaty to an international board with an advisory role to the concerned governments set the stage for this successful negotiation. It assured the governments concerned, federal and local, that their own management responsibilities for the caribou would be respected. Decisions with which they strongly disagreed would not be forced on them by an international body. Without this change in approach, I am convinced that it would not have been possible to conclude an agreement.

Tactically, the decision to go with a single large and decisive negotiating session proved sound. It was also helpful to hold the negotiation at a location convenient to most of the stakeholders and away from the national capitals. We left the meeting in Seattle with representatives of every stakeholder group committed to supporting the draft agreement that we had achieved. In any negotiation, it is essential for the U.S. negotiator to ensure that he has the involvement and full support of the major stakeholders in the issues under consideration. The inclusion in that meeting of Buff Bohlen, a widely respected conservationist, also proved useful. He was not viewed as a partisan advocate for any of the interest groups involved and was able to play an effective role in helping broker the compromises that were necessary to bring the negotiation to a conclusion.

Continued Controversy over ANWR

Since the negotiation of the agreement, oil and gas development in ANWR has remained a contentious subject. The executive and legislative branches of the U.S. government have been unable to agree on whether to go forward with such development. The government of Canada has remained consistently opposed to it on the basis that it would involve unacceptable risk to the Porcupine caribou herd.

It is questionable whether it would now be useful to consider this sensitive and politically charged decision at a meeting of the International Porcupine Caribou Board established by the agreement. Consideration of this matter within the board would likely result in intensified conflict and an impasse on the issue. To avoid such fruitless confrontation, no meeting of the full board has been scheduled since 2001.

The Porcupine Caribou Technical Committee formed under the board has, however, continued to function and address other matters affecting the herd. Moreover, should the United States decide to proceed with oil and gas development in ANWR, Canada would be so informed under the terms of the agreement. At that point, I am confident that the board would play a significant role in the consideration of mitigating measures to limit the risk to the herd.

chapter 5

The U.S.-USSR Science Agreement

C ultural and scientific exchanges took place between the USSR and the United States from the 1950s to the dissolution of the former in December 1991. The Soviets valued the window that such exchanges provided into the more advanced U.S. industrial society. The United States found the exchanges useful in gaining insight into developments in the more closed and secretive USSR (Union of Soviet Socialist Republics).

Notwithstanding their antagonistic relationship, the two Cold War rivals entered into a science and technology agreement in 1972 to facilitate scientific exchanges. The agreement was renewed in 1977; however, in the face of rising Cold War tensions, it was allowed to lapse in 1982. The Soviet invasion of Afghanistan at the end of 1979, for example, had made cooperation under such an agreement untenable for the United States.

The U.S.-USSR relationship went through ups and downs during the Cold War. Throughout that era, however, the United States sought to maintain, to the extent possible, links through which we might have the possibility of exerting some influence on developments in the USSR. U.S. relations with China, our other major Cold War adversary, followed a similar pattern after the opening to China, begun under the Nixon administration in 1971. This differs from a policy of systematically minimizing contacts and seeking to isolate our perceived enemies, which the United States has employed in some other instances (e.g., Cuba, Iran, and North Korea).

In October 1986, President Ronald Reagan and the reformist Soviet leader Mikhail Gorbachev met in Reykjavik, Iceland. By then, the USSR had signaled its intention to phase down its involvement in Afghanistan and eventually withdraw its troops. Cold War tensions had eased considerably. In this improved climate for cooperation, one of the results of the Reykjavik summit was an undertaking by the two leaders to negotiate a science agreement to replace the science and technology agreement that had lapsed in 1982.

To follow up on the Reykjavik summit, the White House Office of Science and Technology Policy (OSTP) led a delegation to Moscow on October 5–6, 1987, for exploratory talks on possible cooperation in the basic sciences. The U.S. delegation included representatives of the State Department, the National Science Foundation (NSF), the U.S. Geological Survey, and the Department of Defense. On the Soviet side, there were officials from the State Committee for Science and Technology, the Soviet Academy of Sciences, the Ministry of Geology, and the Foreign Ministry.

The U.S. delegation to the Moscow meeting presented the concept of a framework agreement under which memoranda of understanding (MOUs) providing the details of particular cooperative science exchanges would be developed between governmental agencies of the two countries. Further, the U.S. delegation made clear that the U.S. interest was in the area of basic science and that we would not consider cooperative activities dealing with applied science. The Soviets suggested areas and topics in basic science that would be of interest to them.

Our emphasis on basic science reflected the fact that the USSR excelled in such fields as theoretical physics and mathematics. Thus, we believed that we could benefit at least as much as the Soviets from cooperation in the basic sciences. NSF, a U.S. government agency that provides grants to scientists and researchers, had already received proposals from U.S. applicants for cooperation with their Soviet counterparts.

We were also concerned that cooperation in the area of technology and applied science would carry a greater risk of contributing to the Soviets' industrial and military capabilities. In general, the United States was ahead of the USSR in the industrial applications of advances in science and thus had less to gain from cooperation in this area. One needs to recall that we were entering into this negotiation during a period of considerable anxiety about Soviet military and industrial capabilities and the threat posed by technology transfer. OSTP's attitude toward a science agreement with the USSR reflected this mood.

Negotiating Guidelines

After the exploratory talks in Moscow ended, the United States began to consider the negotiation of a science and technology agreement with the Soviets. Bill Graham, who headed OSTP, was determined that should an agreement be concluded, the balance of benefits from it not favor the USSR to the disadvantage of the United States. To that end, Graham asserted OSTP leadership on behalf of the White House in the interagency process that prepared our negotiating position.

The OSTP-led interagency process continued at an intensive pace through the final months of 1987 and much of the first half of 1988. Frequent meetings took place, often as many as several per month, to deal in detail with all aspects of the coming negotiation with the Soviets. In addition to limiting cooperation to the basic sciences, we were also determined to craft an agreement that would allow us access to Soviet scientists beyond those identified and selected by the government of the USSR.

We wanted a "bottom-up" approach in which scientists and researchers from the two countries would engage in direct contact with each other and then initiate proposals for cooperative research to their governmental agencies, rather than the other way around, as had previously been the case. This would go against the grain for the Soviets, who emphasized tightly enforced centralized control, but the interagency group agreed that the United States should insist on this approach. The negotiating guidelines that emerged from the interagency working group were firm and left little room to accommodate differing views from the Soviet side.

The State Department normally heads government-to-government international negotiations, and I insisted on our prerogative to do so during the negotiations to follow with the Soviets. I provided assurances that the State Department would consider itself bound by the guidelines that had been prepared under OSTP leadership.

In Pursuit of Cooperation

At that time, I was acting assistant secretary of state for the Bureau of Oceans and International Environmental and Scientific Affairs. Assistant Secretary John Negroponte had moved to the White House as deputy to the president's assistant for security affairs, Colin Powell. Given the importance of this negotiation and the president's role in initiating it, I decided that I should head our negotiating team myself. I agreed with my Soviet counterpart, V. I. Yezhkov, deputy chair of the Soviet State Committee for Science and Technology, to hold a weeklong negotiating session in Washington, May 4–12, 1988.

In my opening remarks at the May meeting, which were cleared by all the concerned agencies within the U.S. government, I characterized our upcoming discussion as "a direct continuation of the exploratory talks that took place in Moscow last October." Drawing on our negotiating guidelines, I went on to describe the four areas of importance to us:

> (1) The agreement will only cover basic science. In this area, we concluded last October, there is considerable opportunity for mutual benefit. We want to be very clear on this point so that there is no room for any misunderstanding and that precious discussion time is not wasted.

> (2) The agreement will take the form of a "framework agreement" between the United States Government and the Govern-

ment of the USSR, with the Office of Science and Technology Policy, on the U.S. side, and the State Committee for Science and Technology Policy, on the Soviet side, acting as executive agents. Under this agreement will come subordinate memoranda of understanding between the implementing agencies in each country; thus, the day-to-day operation of the basic sciences agreement will be carried out by the implementing agencies. We would begin with three memoranda of understanding, one between the U.S. National Science Foundation and the Academy of Sciences of the USSR, the second between the U.S. Geological Survey and the Academy of Sciences of the USSR, and the third between the U.S. Geological Survey and the Ministry of Geology of the USSR.

(3) The form of cooperation at the implementing level would consist primarily of cooperative research projects initiated by investigators of the two countries in direct communication with each other. Joint proposals for such projects would be reviewed by both sides and approved upon mutual agreement.

(4) We discussed areas of research to be included in the program. A list of potential areas prepared by the U.S. side in advance of the Moscow meeting was agreed in full. An additional, extensive list of Soviet proposals was also discussed and it was agreed that the U.S. side would take them back to Washington for detailed review.

Interest in the negotiation ran high within the U.S. government, and I brought to the table a large delegation broadly representative of the interagency science community. The 11-member delegation included Michael Marks, assistant director of OSTP, who had represented OSTP and Graham at many of the interagency meetings during which our negotiating guidelines had been developed. In addition to the delegation members, our negotiating team also had 10 advisers drawn from interested government agencies.

The negotiations made good progress. The Soviets recognized early that the positions presented by the United States had been developed in a painstaking interagency process and contained little room for maneuver. Although the Soviets would have much preferred a broader agreement that included applied science, they were prepared to accept our narrower approach, focused on basic science, to get an agreement. Moreover, the Soviets had an interest in bringing the negotiation to an early conclusion, if possible, so that an agreement could be signed by Reagan and Gorbachev at the U.S.-USSR summit meeting scheduled for May 29 to June 2 in Moscow.

By Wednesday, May 11, the day before the meeting was to have ended, we had developed a joint negotiating draft that appeared to be acceptable to both sides. In fact, from the U.S. perspective, I had never been involved in a negotiation in which the U.S. entering position had been so completely accommodated. Every goal in our negotiating guidelines had been achieved.

With the joint negotiating draft in hand, I met with my full delegation. A consensus emerged from our discussion that we had indeed accomplished what we had set out to do. I proposed to return to the negotiation and inform the Soviet side that I was prepared to initial the text, thus committing me to recommend to my government that we sign the agreement.[1] No one on my delegation objected to my doing so.

The next day, Yezhkov, the Soviet head of delegation, told me that he was also prepared to initial the text. We scheduled a meeting for late the following morning at which the initialing would take place.

A Last-Minute Glitch

Early the following morning, Marks came to my office in the State Department to say that OSTP was having second thoughts and wanted me to inform the Soviets that I was no longer prepared to initial the text. The concern, as he explained to me, was that the direct scientist-to-scientist contacts envisioned by the agreement would be counter to U.S. interests. Marks cited a reference in the text to "private sector scientists." He argued that expanded exchanges between U.S. private sector scientists and Soviet scientists, who by definition work for the government, would be unbalanced in favor of the Soviets.

Marks said that he had been in touch with members of my delegation who represented the Department of Defense, the Department of the Interior, and the Office of the U.S. Trade Representative and that they shared OSTP's concern. According to him, they had reconsidered their earlier consent to initialing the text and now agreed with him that it should not be initialed.

I responded that such scientist-to-scientist contacts were an integral part of the bottom-up approach on which we had insisted, in accordance with the OSTP-prepared negotiating guidelines. Those guidelines had been developed during many months of interagency talks, and the United States had succeeded in getting its preferred approach into the agreement on this point. I also reminded him that the agreement made clear that any cooperation between scientists of the two countries must be governed by MOUs between scientific agencies in the two countries.

I told Marks that I was not willing to renege on my commitment to initial the text on the basis that we were now having second thoughts about language that we had agreed to and that was fully consistent with our negotiating guidelines. Our credibility as a negotiating partner would be called into question if I were to do that. Further, a refusal now to initial would reopen the entire negotiation. All that we had accomplished in getting our points accepted would be lost. I told him that I would initial the text, but that when I did so, I would emphasize to the Soviets its ad referendum nature. I would say that certain concerns had been raised by members of the U.S. negotiating team and that these concerns would need to be taken into account as the U.S. government decided whether to sign the agreement in its current form.

Marks was not pleased with my response. He said that my position was unacceptable and that he would report my intransigence to OSTP Director Graham, who felt strongly about this matter. I later received a phone call from Negroponte, Colin Powell's deputy in the White House. He did not directly criticize my decision to initial the agreement, but he did remind me that Graham was a senior White House official whose views needed to be carefully considered.

Late that morning, the Soviet and U.S. delegations gathered

in Room 1105 in the State Department, a large conference room that features a ring-shaped table, for the purpose of initialing the negotiated text. Just before the meeting was to begin, I was called from the room to a nearby phone. The caller was Michael Smith, a senior Foreign Service Officer, who was on loan to the Office of the U.S. Trade Representative.

He began the conversation by announcing that he was putting me on speaker phone so that others—whom he did not identify—could be party to our conversation. He then told me that I needed to tell the Soviets that the negotiated agreement text was unacceptable. Because he had not previously been involved in the negotiation, I asked him why he took that position. He responded that the agreement provided for contacts between scientists that would be to the disadvantage of the United States—the same objection that had been raised earlier that morning by Marks on behalf of OSTP.

I attempted to engage Smith in a discussion of the relevant provisions of the draft agreement to make the case that they furthered U.S. interests. It quickly became apparent to me that he was unfamiliar with the provisions of the agreement. At that point, I told him that I was not persuaded that I should pull back at this late stage and that I intended to proceed as scheduled. He responded emphatically that I could not sign the agreement. I answered that I was not going to sign it, but that I was going to initial it. I then hung up and returned to the conference room and the waiting U.S. and Soviet delegations.

Before initialing the text, I explained that some on the U.S. side still had concerns. I stressed that the draft agreement would be subject to further review within the U.S. government before a decision would be made regarding whether to sign it as it now stood. The Soviet negotiator Yezhkov accepted my caveat and said that he was in a similar position. His recommendation that the agreement be signed would also be subject to high-level review within his government. Yezhkov and I then placed our initials at the bottom of each page of the draft agreement.

Although my decision to proceed with the initialing had exposed me to some sharp criticism, I took comfort in the support that I received from the majority of my delegation, as well as from senior officials in the State Department. Susan Biniaz, who represented the Office of the Legal Advisor at the State Department on my delegation, made clear that there was no legal objection to my initialing the text.

In a letter to me dated May 16, 1988, Secretary of State George Shultz noted that my entire delegation had been behind the draft agreement through the end of the negotiation with the Soviets and had, at that time, agreed to my initialing it. The secretary concluded, "The fact that some of the agencies later backed out after they had already given their consent [to initialing the text] is their problem, not ours."

A Tendentious Press Leak

The draft agreement was initialed on Friday, May 13, 1988. The following Monday, an article about the negotiations appeared in the *Washington Times*. Its author, Gene Grabowski, cited anonymous sources (described as "worried Reagan administration officials") who were concerned that the agreement could be used by the Soviet Union to obtain data directly from American high-tech companies. He quoted one of those anxious officials as saying that I, the U.S. negotiator, had acted hastily and concluded the negotiation on unfavorable terms so that it could be signed at the forthcoming U.S.-USSR summit in Moscow. The source alleged that the U.S. negotiator "has a case of summit fever."[2]

The article mainly consisted of an attack by the anonymous leakers on my handling of the negotiation. Grabowski had, however, called me over the weekend to give me a chance to comment, and his article included a quote from me saying that the draft agreement authorized the preparation of MOUs between scientific agencies in the two governments and that any cooperation between scientists would be governed by the provisions in those MOUs.

I suspected that the press leak had come from members of my delegation who had posed last-minute objections to my initialing the draft agreement. I could think of no one else who would have had both the motivation and the awareness of events in the negotiation to be behind this leak. The argument against the agreement contained in the article was the same one that had been made to me by Marks on the day that I initialed the draft agreement.

I was sufficiently concerned that on May 17, I wrote a memorandum to Robert Dean on the staff of the National Security Council in the White House in which I said, "I am troubled by the article which appeared in the *Washington Times* on Monday which was based on a leak of information—or more correctly misinformation—concerning our negotiations with the Soviets." I questioned whether we could address issues in an orderly way when such leaks were permitted to occur.

An Agreement Revisited

Within a few days of initialing the draft agreement, I was summoned to present the results of the negotiation to an interagency meeting in the Situation Room in the White House. The Situation Room is the conference room used by the president and his close advisers for high-level meetings. In that august setting, I welcomed the supportive presence of Rozanne Ridgway, assistant secretary of state for European and Canadian Affairs. Ridgway, who had earlier served as a deputy assistant secretary in OES, had fully backed my position on initialing the draft agreement, notwithstanding the last-minute concerns that had been raised.

At the White House meeting, I explained that I entered the negotiation with detailed guidelines that had been prepared and vetted over many months under the leadership of OSTP. I said that I was pleased to report that we had achieved all the negotiating goals in those guidelines. I concluded by recommending that we inform the USSR that the United States was prepared to sign the agreement.

As expected, OSTP Director Graham disagreed, saying that the agreement as drafted would encourage unsupervised direct contacts between Soviet and U.S. scientists that would not be in the interest of the United States. He said that there were also other aspects of the agreement that would have to be revisited, such as the lack of a definition of *basic science*. The meeting ended with agreement that he would work with the Department of State to address his concerns.

A couple of days later, I was called by OSTP and told to join Graham in a meeting in Powell's White House office. In that meeting, Graham presented a proposal for changing certain language in the draft agreement. Powell asked me to review Graham's proposal and get back to the White House promptly with my comments.

The Graham draft put more emphasis on the control to be exercised by the two governments, which would circumscribe direct contacts between scientists. I was confident that the Soviets would accept such a modification, but I believed that it raised a problem for the U.S side. For example, the proposed revision included language stating that under applicable MOUs, the USSR and the United States "may allow" the participation of individual scientists as well as scientific institutions, government and nongovernment agencies, and higher educational institutions. This modification would imply that direct contacts between scientists would not be allowed under the MOUs unless the parties to the agreement made a specific decision to allow it.

Such a change in the language of the agreement would undermine the bottom-up approach envisioned in the negotiating guidelines and return us to the top-down approach that characterized the 1972 agreement. NSF had made clear that it would not participate in a program that repeated this fundamental mistake of the 1972 agreement. As one of the principal agencies that would be working with U.S. scientists seeking Soviet counterparts for cooperation, its objection was particularly significant.

In the specific provision dealing with cooperation, the redraft also included a reference to each party's approving cooperation "in accordance with its national laws, regulations and procedures." The draft agreement already had a separate general provision subjecting cooperation under the agreement to national laws and regulations, so the additional reference to them here was redundant. Such redundancy is generally avoided in international agreements because it raises the question of whether the general provision applies with equal force to those other provisions of the agreement in which the reference is not repeated.

Also, the proposed phrase included not only "laws" and "regulations" but also "procedures." However, the procedures that each country uses in deciding whether and how to undertake cooperation is a matter to be decided entirely by that country, and there was no need to put a reference to such procedures in an international agreement. In this case, it would be particularly unhelpful in that we would appear to be affirming Soviet procedures, of which we did not approve.

The inclusion of a definition of *basic science* in the agreement, which was sought by Graham, was counterproductive. Without such a definition, the United States would be free to decide whether any proposed cooperation was in our view in the area of basic science. With it, the Soviets could, in particular instances, argue that the cooperation that they proposed fit within that agreed definition and that the United States should therefore be prepared to consider it. Because there is a gray area between basic and applied science, the omission of a definition would give us more flexibility in drawing the line in particular instances.

At this juncture, Frederick Bernthal was appointed assistant secretary of state for OES. He took over from me as leader of the U.S. side of the negotiation. He worked out the necessary compromises with OSTP, NSF, and the other concerned agencies. Significantly, the language in the Graham proposal saying that the parties "may allow" contacts between individuals was deleted at NSF's insistence. However, OSTP succeeded in including the requirement for a definition of *basic science*, the redundant reference to national laws and regulations, and the reference to procedures.

A New Era of Science Cooperation

In June, Bernthal led a U.S. delegation to Moscow to complete the negotiation of the basic sciences agreement. The Soviet side was wary of our motives for reopening the negotiated text and suspected that we might be signaling reluctance to conclude an agreement. The negotiations extended over several days and were difficult, particularly with regard to our proposal for including a definition of *basic science*. Finally, agreement was reached on the following definition:

> ..."[B]asic scientific research" means theoretical or experimental research having as its objective the acquisition of fuller knowledge or understanding of the elemental principles of phenomena and observable facts; such research extends the knowledge base from which many societal benefits ultimately flow, and, in the framework of this agreement, such research is not designed for the transformation of new discoveries into applied technologies.

The agreed revision of the agreement's principal operative provision read as follows:

> Cooperative activities in the field of basic scientific research under this Agreement will be subject to official approval in each country, and implemented in accordance with their respective international obligations, national laws, regulations and procedures. Such cooperation will be governed by applicable MOUs. Within this framework:
>
>> such cooperation may include the participation of scientific institutions, government and non-government agencies, higher educational institutions, and individual scientists, specialists and researchers (hereinafter referred to as "partners");
>>
>> partners may carry out such cooperation in approved areas through direct contacts and arrangements.
>
> In order to facilitate implementation of this Agreement, partners of one country intending to visit partners of the other country for purposes of developing or implementing cooperation under this Agreement are to so indicate in applying for permission to enter.

Thus, the Soviets ultimately accepted our proposed modifications to the initialed text. Those modifications did not make any fundamental change in the way in which the agreement would operate. In the revised text, the eight agreed areas of cooperation were the following: geosciences, basic scientific research in engineering sciences, scientific problems of the Arctic and the North, life sciences, science policy, chemistry, mathematics, and theoretical physics.

The delay in completing the agreement prevented Reagan and Gorbachev from signing it at their May 29–June 2 summit meeting in Moscow, as they had planned. Reagan announced his approval of the basic sciences agreement on December 23, 1988. At a meeting in Paris on January 8, 1989, Secretary of State Shultz and Soviet Foreign Minister Eduard Shevardnadze signed the agreement, which was entitled "Agreement between the Government of the United States of America and the Government of the Union of Soviet Socialist Republics on Cooperation in Basic Scientific Research." The negotiation of several implementing MOUs between U.S. and Soviet science agencies was promptly begun.

A Durable and Productive Agreement

At the end of 1991, following the breakup of the Soviet Union, the science agreement was reaffirmed as an agreement between the United States and the Russian Federation. In December 2005, that agreement was renewed for a 10-year period. The renegotiation that led to that renewal resulted in text that remained similar to that of the original 1989 agreement.

This U.S.-Soviet basic sciences agreement, which became an agreement between the United States and Russia, has proved to be among the most productive international science agreements that the United States has concluded. Hundreds of cooperative projects have been undertaken under MOUs prepared pursuant to the agreement. As anticipated, the National Science Foundation and the U.S. Geological Survey have been active participants on the U.S. side, and other agencies have also been involved. Surprisingly, however, the highest number of MOUs under the agreement has been entered into by the U.S. Department of Defense.

Negotiating at the End of the Cold War

The difficulties encountered in completing this negotiation stemmed largely from the fact that we were negotiating in the shadow of the Cold War, which remained a dominant consideration in the minds of some senior officials on the U.S. side even as it was winding down. There were disagreements about how genuine and long-lasting were the positive changes being brought in by the reformist Soviet leader Gorbachev. Graham was one of the senior U.S. officials who appeared convinced that the Soviet Union would remain a dangerous adversary.

OSTP, under his leadership, was concerned that whenever a Soviet and a U.S. scientist were in direct contact, there would be a high risk that the exchange would benefit the Soviet Union more than the United States and thus be counter to U.S. security interests. At the same time, however, OSTP had to accept that it was in our interest to have access to the Soviet scientists with whom we wanted to work, not only those scientists identified and selected by the Soviet bureaucracy. The tension between these two concerns was the source of much of the difficulty that we encountered in developing and sustaining a consistent U.S. posture on the issue of direct contacts between scientists. After we had achieved our negotiating goals, OSTP became increasingly uneasy with the degree to which our position encouraged such contacts between scientists.

In retrospect, it appears to have been the right call to have gone ahead with initialing the text after the May negotiating session. Doing so was helpful in ensuring that none of the text, which largely reflected U.S. views, was reopened for revision except for the modest modifications that the United States later proposed.

One of the lessons that this experience reinforced for me is that a negotiator on sensitive and controversial issues has to expect to face some harsh criticism from those on his or her own team whose views and preferences do not prevail. The challenge is to strike the right balance in terms of overall U.S. interests, while giving a fair hearing to the various viewpoints represented on his delegation. In this instance, the need was to assure that a presidential initiative was not frustrated unnecessarily.

chapter 6

Space Station Partnership

A s President Reagan came into office in January 1981, U.S. space policy was in flux. The maiden voyage of the space shuttle, a reusable space vehicle, was scheduled for April. Priorities between manned and unmanned space exploration had not been sorted out, and the future of scientific research in the space program was not clear.

The idea of building a permanent orbiting space station was a dream of the National Aeronautics and Space Administration (NASA), but it was controversial to others. Supporters asserted that a space station would provide a stepping-stone to outer space, allow for testing the effect on astronauts of extended residence in space, and offer a permanent zero-gravity atmosphere for research purposes.

Opponents of the space station argued that it would be an extremely costly venture that could have an unwelcome effect on NASA's budget, constraining the other activities that the agency would be able to undertake. Also, because there is a limit to how much funding the U.S. government is prepared to allocate for research, it might reduce the budgets for other agencies' science and technology activities. Moreover, some in the scientific community were skeptical about the added value of the research that might take place on a space station.

Reagan made a dramatic announcement in his 1984 State of the Union address that brought closure to the controversy over space policy. He used strong language in calling for the building of a space station: "We can reach for greatness again. We can follow our dreams to distant stars, living in and working in space for peaceful, economic, and scientific gain. Tonight, I am directing NASA to develop a permanently manned space station and do it within a decade." The president went on to say,

> A space station will permit quantum leaps in our research in science, [in] communications, in metals, and in lifesaving medicines which could be manufactured only in space. We want our friends to help us meet these challenges and share in their benefits. NASA will invite other countries to participate so we can strengthen peace, build prosperity, and expand freedom for all who share our goals.

Reagan's announcement triggered a long and complex set of space station talks over the next four years. NASA met frequently with the space agencies in Canada and Japan and with the European Space Agency (ESA), representing nine European countries. Parallel government-to-government meetings, headed on the U.S. side by the State Department, were also held. As the talks and subsequent negotiations progressed, these meetings were often held concurrently. An intense series of interagency meetings was also held to develop the U.S. negotiating strategy and adjust it in response to developments in the negotiations with our partner countries.

Beginnings of a Complicated Negotiation

Responding to the 1984 presidential initiative, NASA promptly set out to complete the conceptual work on what the space station might look like, which it termed "Phase A" of the space station project. At the same time, NASA began talks with its foreign counterparts on subsequent phases. By summer 1985, NASA had completed the negotiation of MOUs with ESA and the space agencies in Canada and Japan. The MOUs defined exactly what the space station would consist of and dealt with the necessary design work. This phase of the project, termed "Phase B," required many meetings and extensive interaction among the cooperating space agencies and was completed in fall 1987.

During this NASA-managed Phase B, decisions were made about what hardware each of the partners would contribute to the space station. The United States would provide the truss structure that would hold all the pieces together, the power systems, and some other basic infrastructure systems. The United States would also build the habitation module that would be the living quarters for the astronauts.

The European, Japanese, and U.S. contributions would each include a laboratory module as part of the main base station. The Europeans would also supply certain detached orbiting elements. The Canadians would provide a mobile servicing system (known as "Canadarm"), based on technology they had contributed to the space shuttle. The system would be used in the assembly and maintenance of the space station and in servicing payloads. These contributions were valued at $16 billion (United States), $4.2 billion (Europe), $2 billion (Japan), and $1 billion (Canada). The use of station resources by each partner was to be allocated roughly in accordance with its anticipated contribution.

Talks covering the later phases of the project, which included the building, operation, and cooperative use of the space station, had also begun during this period. These talks took place both between NASA and each of its counterpart space agencies and among representatives of all the governments concerned.

As principal deputy assistant secretary for the Bureau of Oceans and International Environmental and Scientific Affairs, I chaired the first government-to-government meeting with the Europeans, held in Washington in November 1985. Reinhard Loosch, a deputy assistant secretary in the German Foreign Ministry, headed the European delegation, representing the nine participating governments. He was a seasoned and loquacious diplomat who kept his large multinational delegation operating smoothly. His positive attitude and his ability to keep the conversation going even when we appeared to be at an impasse were helpful throughout the negotiating process.

Loosch made it clear at the European-U.S. meeting in November that Europe considered it essential to have an intergovernmental agreement that dealt with these later phases of the project, as well as MOUs between NASA and each of its partner space agencies. His argument, which the U.S. side accepted, was that on such an important and long-term commitment, an agreement among the governments concerned was needed, in addition to the arrangements worked out among participating space agencies. After similar exchanges with Canada and Japan, talks began on both the agreement among the concerned governments and the MOUs among the space agencies.

One issue that needed to be addressed was what form the intergovernmental agreement should take. A treaty, which would require Senate consent for ratification, could be helpful in demonstrating that we were making a permanent commitment and had the backing of Congress. For that reason, our partners expressed a preference for a treaty approach. On the other hand, there was some concern that the Senate's required two-thirds vote in favor of a treaty might be difficult to obtain or, at least, that the ratification process could involve delays that would interfere with the timely initiation of the space station project. The president arguably had the authority to engage in this kind of cooperative venture without a treaty. However, because the project would require large congressional appropriations over a long period, a case could also be made that a treaty was needed.

At this juncture, Congress announced its intent to insert language in NASA's budget authorization for 1988 calling for any governmental agreement on space station cooperation to be placed before the Congress for 30 days before going into effect. This legislative language gave us confidence that any type of agreement would be subject to appropriate congressional review and have adequate support in Congress before entering into force. Thus, the balance was tipped in favor of making the intergovernmental agreement an executive agreement. Such an agreement could be put into effect by the executive branch without the formal advice and consent of the Senate, as would be required in the case of a treaty. This approach was acceptable to our negotiating partners.

Beginning in 1986, as we moved from general talks to begin the actual negotiation of an agreement, Bob Morris, the deputy assistant secretary for science in OES, headed our delegations to a series of government-to-government talks. He had recently returned from a tour as science attaché at the U.S. embassy in Germany.

Peggy Finarelli, director of NASA's Space Station Policy Division, who had negotiated the MOUs covering Phase B, led the U.S. side in parallel meetings with our partners' space agencies on the MOUs that would cover these later phases of the project. During these two sets of meetings, the partners came to grips with the complexity of the undertaking and blocked out the kinds of provisions that would be needed in the agreement and the MOUs, such as provisions on shared use, management of the space station, applicable legal regimes, liability, and technology transfer.

A Call for Negotiating Guidelines

In November 1986, Frank Gaffney, Jr., assistant secretary of defense for security policy, called an urgent meeting at the Pentagon of representatives of all U.S. agencies taking part in the space station talks. This took Morris and me by surprise because the Department of Defense had thus far not been an active participant in the process, having stated that it had no plans to make use of a space station. However, Gaffney made it clear in this meeting that from that point forward, Defense would be determined to ensure that its potential interests be fully taken into account.

As I listened to him, I became convinced that Defense would prefer that any space station be a solely U.S. national asset so that the department would have broad flexibility in making use of it should it choose to do so. In any case, Defense was committed to making sure that our right to make national security uses of any international station was protected. It is worth noting that this meeting was taking place at a time when the Strategic Defense Initiative, often referred to as "Star Wars," was under consideration by the Reagan administration. This had implications regarding possible defense-related research and development uses that might be made of a space station.

At the end of this meeting, I reluctantly concluded that Defense would not be disappointed if an attempt at international cooperation in building and operating a space station failed. I viewed this difference in perspective between Defense and State as consistent with the institutional biases of the two government agencies: State generally stresses the advantages of international cooperation, while Defense tends to put greater value on the increased flexibility and control that come with acting alone.

Gaffney pressed for a full review of all aspects of our negotiating position, concentrating on the intergovernmental agreement. He insisted on developing comprehensive negotiating guidelines to be approved by the president. As a result, an interagency working group was established for this purpose.

It was agreed that after the guidelines had been prepared and approved, the working group would remain in existence to provide continuing guidance to the U.S. team as the negotiations among the concerned governments went forward. The State Department accepted an interagency working group with this mandate on the condition that it would be led by OES. I chaired this group.

The newly established interagency working group reported to the White House through Ty Cobb, who handled space issues on the National Security Council (NSC) staff. A disciplined and well-respected former Army officer, he made sure that interagency differences were fairly considered and cleanly and expeditiously resolved. He was prepared to present options to the president for decision when necessary to break interagency deadlocks. He also stepped in to chair the working group meetings on a couple of occasions when the agenda included an issue for decision over which State and Defense were sharply divided. The competence he displayed and the confidence he inspired were essential elements in keeping the negotiations moving forward at several critical junctures.

Ted Williams, who represented the Department of Energy, and Cobb regularly attended meetings of the interagency working group that I chaired. At one such session, I observed that any baseball fan would agree that having both Ty Cobb and Ted Williams on our side should give us confidence that we had a winning team.

Two negotiating issues were of central importance: the need for the United States to be able to make appropriate national security uses of the space station and to obtain the partners' recognition and acceptance of that, and the need for the United States to have overall operational control of the space station. Also, it was viewed as essential that the project provide for a core U.S. space station that could be capable of autonomous operation without the partners' participation.

In mid-February 1987, the interagency group completed its work, and the president signed a set of negotiating guidelines. By then, our partners were troubled by the extended pause in our talks with them, and they were particularly upset that the guidelines introduced the national security issue into the negotiation of the intergovernmental agreement. During this time, the concern about national security uses had been picked up by the press, both in the United States and in Canada, Europe, and Japan, and was becoming a major media issue.

The national security uses issue was especially difficult to deal with because we had no specific examples to give of such intended uses. We acknowledged that any such uses would have to be consistent with the peaceful purposes to which the space station was to be dedicated. This would obviously preclude the stationing of offensive weapons on the station; however, for example, it was not clear whether, or what kinds of, weapons research might be permitted on the space station. Essentially, it came down to a question of who would decide whether a particular use of the space station was for peaceful purposes.

Proposed Draft and Negotiating Strategy

On the basis of the presidential guidelines, a negotiating draft of an intergovernmental agreement was prepared that laid out our preferred positions in stark, hard-line fashion. The working group developed a negotiating strategy with the following major elements:

(1) Hold separate government-to-government negotiations with Canada, Europe, and Japan, which would parallel MOU talks between NASA and each of the cooperating space agencies, and bring the pieces together into a comprehensive intergovernmental agreement at a later stage.

(2) Seek to focus discussion on our proposed text for an intergovernmental agreement as the basic negotiating document.

(3) Be prepared to be flexibile on the presentation of the agreement while holding firm to the substance of our positions.

A multilateral meeting—not a negotiating session—was held with all the partners in Washington in February 1987 to present and explain our new intergovernmental negotiating text. Our partners were dismayed at its uncompromising nature, particularly the direct and specific reference it contained to national security uses of the space station. They went home angry. This was clearly a low point in the negotiation, and it was not obvious how the barriers to agreement that then existed could be overcome.

Preparation to Negotiate

David Colson, who was then the State Department's assistant legal adviser for OES, had for some time been expressing to both OES Assistant Secretary John Negroponte and me his growing concern that the space station venture was in trouble. He cautioned that if it failed, OES—as the lead bureau in the negotiation—would be blamed for failing to deliver on a major presidential initiative. Colson strongly urged that OES elevate the level of its involvement and make every effort to ensure that the negotiations conclude successfully.

Negroponte shared Colson's concerns and asked that I take over as chief U.S. negotiator. I agreed that having chaired the interagency review of our negotiating guidance, I was in the best position to lead the U.S. side in the government-to-government negotiations. In taking on this task, I recognized how difficult it would be to maintain a consensus on our negotiating approach within my own delegation while seeking to bridge the differences that remained between the United States and its space station partners.

Anticipating a tough interagency battle ahead, I was sure that I would need all the leverage that I could get, so I took steps to formally establish my position as official head of the U.S. negotiating team. At my request, Assistant Secretary Negroponte asked Secretary of State Shultz to designate me as chief negotiator and send that designation by letter to Secretary of Defense Caspar Weinberger, NASA Administrator James Fletcher, and the president's national security advisor, Frank Carlucci.

On March 3, 1987, Deputy Secretary John Whitehead, who was acting secretary of state at the time, sent a letter to Weinberger, Fletcher, and Carlucci welcoming the renewal of the government-to-government negotiations and asking for their help in achieving "one of the largest and most visionary international cooperative ventures ever undertaken." He went on to designate me as the chief negotiator for these negotiations, adding that I had his full confidence.

A Controversial Move

In the next round of meetings with each of the partners, I engaged in genuine negotiations and responded sympathetically to their concerns. In the process, I signaled the possibility of more flexibility in our position than Defense representatives on my delegation thought was appropriate. Following these negotiations, I shepherded through the backstopping interagency working group a revised negotiating draft of the intergovernmental agreement.

The revised draft showed some significant movement toward

our partners' positions. This included the removal of the reference
to national security uses in the agreement itself in return for a
proposed separate "agreed minute" dealing with the negotiating
history on this point. The agreed minute would make clear that
the negotiators envisioned national security uses that were consistent with the peaceful purposes of the space station.

Although I viewed these changes as fully protecting U.S. interests, they were extremely controversial within my own delegation.
Defense vigorously resisted any show of flexibility, especially the
removal of the national security reference from the intergovernmental agreement. Defense's concern was that a separate agreed
minute was less visible and could get buried in the future, thus
constituting a less clear agreement to national security uses of the
space station.

This conflict between State and Defense went to the NSC staff
for resolution, and Cobb decided that the changes in the revised
draft were acceptable and consistent with the presidential guidelines. We came within hours of taking the issue to the president
before Defense agreed to go along with the NSC decision. The
Defense representatives remained unhappy with Cobb's decision.
I suspect that they agreed to accept the revised draft because they
were not confident that a decision by Reagan would have gone
their way.

A Bombshell from the Defense Department

In early April 1987, as the revised negotiating draft was being
approved, Secretary of Defense Weinberger dropped a bombshell
in the form of a letter to Shultz. The letter, which was promptly
leaked to the press, said that the United States "must be prepared
to go forward alone" unless its allies were prepared to give the
Department of Defense broad latitude to "conduct national security activities on U.S. elements of the space station."

Weinberger warned Shultz to avoid "paying too high a price
for international cooperation." An April *New York Times* article
by David Sanger, datelined April 9, 1987, noted that the letter

became public "just as the Reagan Administration was trying to quell fears from Canada, Japan, and the European Space Agency that the space station was evolving from a civilian project into a military one."[1]

Using our contacts at every level, the U.S. negotiating team undertook a damage control effort aimed at reassuring our partners that our offer of cooperation on a civilian space station for peaceful purposes was still in play. For example, Shultz sent the following letter to Canadian Secretary of State for External Affairs Joe Clark:

> Thank you for your letter of April 10 noting Defense Secretary Weinberger's recent letter regarding the Space Station negotiations and urging that the U.S. stand by the original terms of its invitation to Canada to participate in the Space Station program. Let me assure you that the President's original invitation to Canada to cooperate with the United States in building and operating a civil Space Station on the basis of genuine partnership is unchanged. The letter of then NASA Administrator James Beggs dated April 6, 1984, to which you referred, reflects the letter and spirit of that invitation.
>
> We recognize that the national security use issue, which has been the subject of continuing discussions between the U.S. and Canadian delegations in the Space Station negotiations, is of major importance to Canada. Our delegation is prepared to discuss it further during the next round of talks in Ottawa. We have already provided to the Canadian delegation a revised draft agreement that we hope will be viewed by Canada as constructive movement in handling this and other issues. I am confident that we will be able to find solutions that protect the interests of both Canada and the United States, so that cooperation on this exciting endeavor can go forward to the benefit of both countries.

Another Difficult Round

Based on our hard-fought revision of the negotiating text, we held another round of talks with each of our negotiating partners in spring and early summer 1987. These were difficult sessions and quickly got down to the hard issues on which we had little or no remaining room to negotiate. These dealt mainly with how operational issues would be managed in the absence of consensus, including with respect to national security uses. Our meeting with the Japanese was especially troublesome. We ended that meeting without, for the first time, being able to agree on a date for a subsequent meeting—not a good omen in any negotiation.

The Europeans asserted that what we were proposing did not amount to the genuine partnership that had been offered by the president. We countered that we had repeatedly shown flexibility and were getting nothing in return. Our partners needed to recognize and accept that we were putting out bottom-line positions. Time was running out. We planned to move into the next phases of developing and building the space station soon, with or without partners.

The chair of ESA's Council of Ministers wrote to Reagan to express Europe's deep concern. Reagan's response was brief—but reassuring—about the partnership offer, expressed confidence in the negotiations, and did not get into a substantive discussion of the remaining issues.

The President's Decision

On the basis of the latest round of negotiations, I proposed to draft a new negotiating text that would seek to respond to some of the concerns raised by our partners. I knew that this proposal would encounter strong resistance within my delegation, but I was convinced that without a new text, the negotiations were headed toward certain failure. The Department of Defense did indeed strongly oppose the writing of any new draft that would show additional flexibility.

Defense asserted that I had already exceeded my mandate and gone beyond what I should have done by compromising on our agreed negotiating positions. Defense representatives insisted that any decision on whether to prepare a new draft would have to go to the president. They agreed, however, that if a decision to go forward with a new text were made by the president, they would accept the NSC staff as the arbitrators of the particular changes to be made.

The NSC, with Cobb taking the lead, presented the issue for presidential decision. Reagan decided that we should prepare a new text as a basis for further talks with our negotiating partners. The new text was prepared for the first time in multilateral form suitable for negotiation with all our partners together, rather than one at a time as we had been doing.

In addition to some minor changes desired by our partners, the new text included two highly significant changes: the right for each provider of a user element, such as the laboratory modules, to decide what uses of it would meet the "peaceful purposes" criterion, and a commitment that in its evolution the space station would remain a civil station for peaceful purposes.

Although they represented a shift in the approach we were taking to protect our interests, these changes in our position still were designed to meet Defense's primary concern. The United States would maintain its right to decide what national security uses would be allowable in a space station devoted to peaceful purposes—at least with respect to the space station user elements that the United States provided.

In September 1987, to explain the new text to each of our partners, we held one final round of separate talks with Canada, Europe, and Japan. I also used the occasion of these talks to discuss other areas of concern raised by them and agreed to consider whether certain further changes might be possible. Again, the Defense representatives on my delegation were unhappy. The senior Defense representative on the delegation, Philip Kunsberg, asserted that I was not presenting the latest draft as the "final offer" text that Defense believed that it was intended to be. Although I recognized that my remaining negotiating room was extremely limited, I still viewed the draft as a negotiating text. I was not willing to present this text as an ultimatum, as Defense apparently would have preferred.

The Final Push to Partnership

A multilateral meeting that included all the partners was held in Washington in October 1987. It was an intense negotiating session at which we produced a new draft that included some relatively minor further changes. At this point, I made clear that I had used all my negotiating flexibility and considered the negotiation to be virtually concluded. The legal experts group, which had been meeting since August, had not yet reached final agreement on a legal annex or on certain legal provisions, such as those dealing with technology transfer and liability. We agreed that the final text of the intergovernmental agreement would include articles on these topics based on the completed work of the legal experts group. We left the meeting with the understanding that Canada, Europe, and Japan would now reflect on whether we had achieved an acceptable basis for continued cooperation on an international space station.

Certain of the major issues remained less than fully resolved and were discussed further between my negotiating counterparts and me during the months that followed. On the disruptive issue of national security uses, the partners had agreed that each of us could use our space station elements for peaceful purposes in accordance with international law, consistent with our own determination of what constitutes "peaceful purposes." However, they continued to find this point's inclusion in the agreement text or in an agreed minute too formal a way of covering it. The Japanese delegation, headed by Hidehiko Hamada (assistant director of the Scientific Affairs Division in the United Nations Bureau in Japan's Ministry of Foreign Affairs), supported Loosch in insisting that this approach was unacceptable.

It was apparent to me that our negotiating partners accepted that some national security activities by the United States, and probably by some other partner countries as well, would take place on the space station. Their concern was that if the national security aspect of this cooperative venture were too prominently featured, it would cast a shadow on the "peaceful purposes" commitment. Further, it would cause them problems with their own publics and media critics.

After some further back-and-forth on this issue, it was agreed that the problem could be resolved through an exchange of letters between me and the chief negotiators for Europe and Japan. This exchange would cover the negotiating history and make clear that there was an understanding on how the "peaceful purposes" provision would be interpreted. This conclusion was reached after extensive consideration of the standing and weight that could be given to such an exchange of letters between negotiators, compared with language contained in the text of an agreement.

Canada was a special problem. It was building a remote control arm that would provide services to all the partners. Since this was a "critical path" part of the space station infrastructure, Canada could not exercise control over the purposes for which its element would be used, as could the other partners. William "Mack" Evans, the Canadian negotiator and head of the Canadian space program, sought assurance that Canada could withdraw from the space station venture at any time, with adequate compensation, should it conclude that an intended use of the arm was unacceptable. Ultimately, we agreed to give Canada this assurance.

The remaining contentious point dealt with the critical issue of operational control of the space station. The Europeans were not comfortable with having language in the intergovernmental agreement specifying that NASA would have the last word on coordination and direction, including with respect to Europe's separate elements. We could not give ground on the substance of this issue because NASA's ability to make operational decisions for the whole space station in the absence of consensus was absolutely essential. Indeed, our negotiating guidelines from the beginning made clear that NASA had to have this authority. The question then became whether and how we could protect NASA's role in this regard without causing Europe to back away from the agreement.

This issue had been for some time a source of disagreement within the U.S. delegation. In accordance with the MOUs, all operational decisions were to be vetted through a NASA-controlled decisionmaking body, the Space Station Control Board (SSCB). Although control boards normally operate under the consensus principle, NASA, as chair, preserved its right to make decisions in the absence of consensus. NASA believed that this adequately protected its ability to exercise its responsibility for operational management of the station. Others on my delegation took the position that specific language on this point was needed in the intergovernmental agreement. They argued that a reference in the intergovernmental agreement was necessary to show more clearly that our partner countries accepted this principle of NASA operational control.

I was not convinced that Europe could be persuaded to agree to a specific reference in the intergovernmental agreement to NASA's ultimate decisionmaking role regarding Europe's own elements, even though they agreed to it in practice by accepting that the SSCB had that authority. In the end, I concluded that the agreement that the board would make operational decisions would be fully consistent with the presidential guidance calling for U.S. control of space station design, development, operation, and utilization. It would provide for our ability to make unilateral decisions when necessary. I was concerned that if we were to insist not only on the substance of our position but also on expressing it in ways that were unpalatable to our partners, this international cooperative venture would not be possible. I agreed, therefore, to the absence of such language from the intergovernmental agreement.

Thus, we finally were able to reach agreement on all the remaining issues and bring the negotiation to a successful conclusion. To some, it might appear that I had compromised too much to achieve this result. I was and remain convinced that I fully protected our essential positions. From the beginning, we negotiated from texts that the U.S. side prepared, and we controlled the negotiating agenda. The concessions that I made were largely presentational. For example, although we would have preferred to have language in the text on national security uses, our position on this issue was protected by the exchange of letters between the negotiators. Moreover, I believe that the accommodations we made to the views of our partners were necessary for this cooperative project to take place.

A signing ceremony was held in the State Department's elegant

Benjamin Franklin Room late in the afternoon on September 29, 1988. Earlier that afternoon, Finarelli and I briefed the press at the State Department. Her explanation of the agreements to be signed gives a good sense of the complexity of the undertaking:

> Now, let me describe the agreements a little bit. The structure of the agreements that we have is, first of all, an intergovernmental agreement, or IGA. So the signatories are the government of the United States, and Secretary Shultz will be signing for the United States, the government of Canada, the government of Japan, and the nine European governments who are participating in the program. The Europeans participate through the European Space Agency—that's their technical agency that works on the program; but it's the European governments who are participating in the program who will be signing the IGA.
>
> This IGA is an umbrella framework that has statements about broad principles of cooperation, and it also provides the legal regime under which we'll be operating up there in orbit.
>
> Underneath this umbrella framework, we have three agency-level memoranda of understanding, and those are naturally between NASA and ESA, between NASA and Canada, and NASA and Japan. Today we will be signing two of those MOUs—the MOU with ESA and the MOU with the Canadians. We will not be signing the MOU with Japan today; the Japanese have to go through an internal process whereby their Diet ratifies the IGA and then they will be able to sign the MOU. So the signature will be of the two MOUs today.
>
> The MOUs are standard fare in cooperative programs in the science and engineering area. They provide all of the programmatic details, the technical details, schedules, management, that type of thing—quite detailed agreements.

She noted that we had been negotiating on this project for more than two and a half years. She explained that the space station would be a major component of the space programs of each of the partners and that we had to produce a package that simultaneously satisfied the policy interests and needs of all of them. It was not an easy job.

It was with a sense of elation that I attended the signing

ceremony and the reception that followed. In this formal setting, representatives of each of the countries involved signed the "Agreement among the Government of the United States of America, Governments of Member States of the European Space Agency, the Government of Japan, and the Government of Canada on Cooperation in the Detailed Design, Development, Operation, and Utilization of the Permanently Manned Civil Space Station."

The drama of the occasion was heightened by the remarkable coincidence that earlier that same day, NASA had successfully launched space shuttle Discovery, marking our first return to space since the disastrous explosion of space shuttle Challenger in January 1986.

My satisfaction at what had been achieved was reinforced when I received a note dated October 24, 1988, from Secretary Shultz, who wrote that the signing of the space station agreements "marked a new era in international cooperation in space." He called the launching of this cooperative venture a "historic feat." On the subject of negotiating, Shultz once gave me some useful advice. He told me that he was always prepared to accept a more extended pause in a conversation than his negotiating partner. He said that it was amazing what people would say just to break the silence.

This historic cooperative space project went forward, and a permanently manned space station is in orbit and is operational. The partner countries are putting in place the final elements to complete the station as envisioned. Following the fall of the USSR and the end of the Cold War, the Russian Federation was brought into the partnership, and when the Columbia space shuttle was lost on February 1, 2003, a Russian space vehicle was employed as a stopgap measure until the shuttles were returned to service.

Elements of a Successful Negotiation

A number of factors contributed to keeping this negotiation alive, even though it often teetered on the brink of failure. For example, NASA's long history of fruitful international cooperation with our partners' space agencies was of major importance. In that context, Finarelli's forceful leadership of the MOU negotiations was very helpful. She was able to keep the talks between the space agencies moving forward even when the government-to-government negotiations were faltering, which kept us from losing momentum on the overall effort.

Another central factor contributing to the success of this negotiation was our ability to get decisions made when necessary in the face of interagency disagreement. It helped that I headed both the negotiating team and the interagency group that developed our negotiating instructions. Moreover, I did so with the express support of both Assistant Secretary Negroponte and Secretary Shultz, which reinforced my position when I had to confront Defense during some tough interagency disputes.

In getting those decisions made, the importance of an engaged and effective NSC staff in the White House can hardly be overstated. When the interagency process deadlocked, we could depend on Ty Cobb at the NSC to step in to resolve the dispute. When necessary, he did not hesitate to present an issue to the president for decision so that we could keep moving forward. Timely decisions that cleanly resolved interagency disputes were not something that, from my experience in previous administrations, could be taken for granted.

The way we structured the negotiations, though seemingly awkward and time-consuming, also worked in our favor. The extended period of bilateral negotiations with each of our partners allowed us to sort out and resolve problems more efficiently than if we had tried to negotiate multilaterally from the beginning.

Also significant was the unfailing congressional support that we had. We sustained this support by meeting with the staff of concerned House and Senate committees before and after every negotiating session. I was completely open with them, laying out the negotiating hurdles that we were facing and how we planned to get over them. We treated Congress like a part of the negotiating team and were thus able to build a reservoir of trust and confidence. As a result, even though we were making a commitment to spend billions of dollars in future congressional appropriations,

—Carl Stoiber

there was no criticism from Congress when we announced agreement, and some members sent supportive letters.

The following is an excerpt from a letter dated October 14, 1988, to NASA Administrator Fletcher, which was jointly signed by Senator Ernest Hollings (South Carolina), chair of the Senate Committee on Commerce, Science, and Transportation, and Senator Donald Riegle, Jr. (Michigan), chair of that committee's Subcommittee on Science, Technology, and Space:

> We would like to note that we are able to provide this endorsement for these agreements in an expedited manner because of the continuous dialogue we have had throughout the negotiating process with NASA and the Department of State. The willingness of NASA and Department negotiating teams to consult with us and to keep us informed of the status and substance of the discussions has been a very positive experience and has been greatly appreciated by the Committee.

The fact that we were dealing with a presidential initiative—announced in a State of the Union address and repeated at several multilateral summit meetings—worked in our favor. With President Reagan so firmly and publicly committed to the project, failure of the negotiation was not an attractive option.

chapter 7

Human Rights and the Environment

Would I agree to head the U.S. delegation to a meeting of the Conference on Security and Co-operation in Europe (CSCE)? It was early summer 1989, and the question came from Deputy Assistant Secretary Avis Bohlen in the State Department's Bureau of European and Canadian Affairs. The meeting would deal with environmental issues and was scheduled to take place from October 16 to November 3 in Sofia, Bulgaria. I jumped at the opportunity.

CSCE brought together East-West Cold War adversaries.[1] It came into being on August 1, 1975, in Helsinki, Finland, when heads of 35 nations signed the Final Act of the Conference on Security and Co-operation in Europe. The agreement was aimed at the avoidance of conflict, a worthy objective given the potential of Cold War tensions to explode in nuclear conflict. Soviet leader Leonid Brezhnev termed the agreement "a victory of reason" and "a gain for all who cherish peace and security on our planet." Importantly, the agreement also confirmed human rights as an appropriate issue to be addressed by the countries concerned.

Further, the Helsinki Final Act called for cooperation across a broad range of issues, which were grouped into three categories, or "baskets": (1) questions relating to security in Europe; (2) cooperation in the fields of economics, science and technology, and the environment; and (3) cooperation in humanitarian and other fields.

The Environment–Human Rights Nexus

The 1989 Sofia meeting was the first gathering of CSCE countries that would deal with a basket 2 issue, the environment. The meeting provided an opportunity to get the Communist countries, which had been notoriously neglectful of environmental pollution concerns, more engaged in efforts to deal with global environmental problems. The agenda for the meeting included the transboundary effects of water pollution and industrial accidents and the management of hazardous chemicals.

Bulgaria's human rights record clouded the outlook for the Sofia meeting. An especially troubling problem was the country's oppression of its Turkish minority: ethnic Turks in Bulgaria were prohibited from speaking Turkish and were discouraged from practicing their Islamic religion. Many ethnic Turks were hounded into migrating to Turkey, often dividing families. It was estimated that more than 310,000 ethnic Turks had fled Bulgaria in response to that country's policy of repression and forced assimilation. Bulgaria turned aside Turkey's overtures to meet to resolve these problems. As a result, Turkey announced its intention not to attend the CSCE meeting in Sofia.

This presented a serious dilemma for the United States and the other CSCE states. The Bulgarian human rights violations were profoundly disturbing and could not be ignored. At the same time, countries' pulling out of CSCE meetings for whatever reason could undermine the CSCE process itself, which had proved valuable in dealing with East-West issues. It had, for example, provided an agreed forum where human rights concerns could be addressed.

In the Vienna CSCE meeting that had concluded the previous January, all 35 CSCE member states had committed to attending the Sofia meeting, laying down no conditions other than the openness and access common to all CSCE meetings. The United States thus decided, notwithstanding some serious misgivings on the part of U.S. human rights activists, that it should attend the meeting and do what it could to persuade Turkey to reconsider its decision not to attend. My argument to Turkey was that empty chairs have no voices.

In addition to addressing the environmental issues on the agenda, we planned to use U.S. attendance at the meeting as a chance to express our displeasure with Bulgaria's human rights practices, particularly its harsh treatment of its Turkish minority. In effect, we would be pursuing two parallel sets of talks—one on the environment and the other on human rights. As a sign of concern about Bulgaria's human rights practices, the United States, as well as most other CSCE countries, would be represented at a lower level than had been usual at other CSCE meetings. It was as a result of that consideration that I, a deputy assistant secretary, rather than a more senior official, headed the U.S. delegation.

Preparations for Sofia

The Turkish minority issue was causing discomfort for Bulgaria and Turkey. Both countries were encountering problems as a result of the disorderly exodus of ethnic Turks from Bulgaria to Turkey. Bulgaria, however, had not been willing to enter into talks with Turkey to seek a solution. There seemed to be little prospect that the Bulgarian government, led by an entrenched Stalinist dictator, Todor Zhivkov, would back down on its efforts to forcibly assimilate the country's ethnic Turks.

Our leverage with Bulgaria came from that country's interest in improving its international reputation, particularly in view of its upcoming role as host of the fall meeting. Also, as was becoming obvious to all concerned, including the Bulgarians, the meeting would be taking place in the twilight of the Cold War and of the oppressive Soviet and East European Communist regimes. This added to Bulgaria's sense of isolation on human rights issues.

As a result of the pressure they would come under, both before and during the meeting, there was reason to hope that the Bulgarians could be persuaded to show some flexibility, at least on the more egregious aspects of the country's treatment of its Turkish minority, such as permitting more freedom of worship for Muslims and relaxing restrictions on the speaking of Turkish. Further, Bulgaria might agree to cooperate with Turkey on setting up a more orderly and humane regime for regulating the migration of ethnic Turks.

The United States also had an interest in having the Sofia meeting succeed in meeting its environmental goals. We were engaged in numerous global agreements and negotiations dealing with the transboundary aspects of air and water pollution. First, it was important that what was agreed to in Sofia be consistent with the positions we were currently taking in other forums, such as the Paris-based Organisation for Economic Co-operation and Development (OECD), which had work under way on toxic chemicals and industrial accidents. Second, we wanted to avoid duplicating the work going forward in other forums. Third, we wanted the approaches that had worked well for us—such as those in the Great Lakes Water Quality Agreement between Canada and the United States—to be recognized as useful globally. For all those reasons, we prepared to be an active participant in the environmental discussions that would take place in Sofia.

On September 29, 1989, I testified on the forthcoming CSCE meeting in Sofia before the congressionally established Commission on Security and Cooperation in Europe, chaired by Representative Steny Hoyer (Maryland). In the following excerpt from my testimony, I sought to bring out both the connection between environmental concerns and freedom of expression and the need for international cooperation:

> First, let me emphasize that we see a key linkage between environmental progress and freedom of expression. Individuals and organizations must be free to express their environmental concerns and press to have them addressed or environmental problems will not be solved. This is a central message that we need to bring to Sofia.
>
> Also, we must emphasize that the major environmental problems are not national, but international in character. Pollution knows no national boundaries; insisting that these issues

be addressed cooperatively does not constitute interference in internal affairs. Rather, such insistence is the only way real progress can be made.

I concluded by saying that the Sofia meeting would offer "a unique opportunity to highlight, in an East-West forum, invaluable work on environmental challenges already completed on which we can all draw," as well as "a significant platform to continue voicing our concerns about human rights in Eastern Europe and the Soviet Union." My arguments for participating actively in the Sofia meeting were well received by the committee members.

Determined to play a strong and constructive role in all aspects of the meeting, we put together a large delegation. It included representatives of environmental nongovernmental organizations (NGOs) plus representatives of human rights NGOs, such as the newly combined U.S.-based Human Rights Watch and the U.S. Helsinki Watch. (Helsinki Watch organizations had been set up in some of the CSCE member countries in the West to monitor the follow-up to CSCE's Final Act at the Helsinki meeting.) The delegation also included a substantial cadre of EPA experts capable of addressing any of the environmental issues on the agenda. To emphasize our human rights concerns, Josh Gilder, the principal deputy assistant secretary in the State Department's Bureau of Human Rights and Humanitarian Affairs, was selected as deputy head of delegation.

The Political Committee of the North Atlantic Treaty Organization (NATO) was used as the principal forum to coordinate the views of the Western countries with regard to the Sofia meeting. At a meeting on September 14, 1989, the committee held a wide-ranging discussion of its approach to Sofia. The member countries addressed such questions as the desirability of attendance, the appropriate rank of the heads of its delegations, its attitude toward a concluding document, and the role of NGOs. Most delegations, including the United States, appealed to Turkey to reconsider its decision not to attend, arguing that it would be damaging to the CSCE process should any Western country opt out. The Turkish delegate defended Turkey's position by saying that it should not be business as usual in the face of such egregious human rights violations on the part of a CSCE host country. He agreed, however, to report our appeals for Turkey's attendance to his government in Ankara.

Most delegations confirmed that their countries would be represented at the Sofia meeting not at the ministerial level, but rather by diplomats and environmental experts. The U.S. representative agreed that ministerial representation would not be appropriate, given the unfortunate human rights situation in Bulgaria. Some delegates spoke in favor of having a concluding document in Sofia. The U.S. delegate responded that it was too early to reach a decision on this point. We wanted to be clear on what would be included in such a document before making a commitment to have one.

The committee reached consensus on the need to urge Bulgaria to meet its CSCE commitments concerning openness, including access to the meeting for NGOs and the press. Also, there was general agreement that we should not permit the environment-related agenda to limit our expression of concern about human rights violations. The U.S. delegate made clear our intention to raise human rights issues in general statements as well as in connection with various agenda topics, and he urged others to do the same.

On September 28, I had an encouraging meeting in Washington with visiting Bulgarian government officials Boris Chakalov and Todor Churov. They noted with obvious pleasure that Bulgaria would shortly become a signatory to the Montreal Protocol on Substances that Deplete the Ozone Layer and to the Basel Convention on Transboundary Movements of Hazardous Wastes. Chakalov gave strong assurances concerning the Sofia meeting's openness to the public, including environmental NGOs. I asked specifically about Ecoglasnost, a prominent Bulgarian NGO that had been unsuccessful in its efforts to obtain recognition by the Bulgarian government. I was told that its members would be given access to the meeting in their personal capacity.

I stressed to the Bulgarian officials our concern for the integrity of the overall CSCE process and, in that context, our view of the appropriateness of raising human rights issues. They did not object to this, but did note that it might open the door for other delegations to raise other, unspecified issues not on the agenda that we would not welcome. They also said that it might give rise to a point of order requiring the Bulgarian chair of the meeting to make a ruling on the question of the germaneness of human rights issues.

The Sofia Meeting

I arrived in Sofia with 10 members of my delegation on a lovely fall day, Sunday, October 15, 1989. That evening, U.S. Ambassador Sol Polansky hosted a reception at his residence for the delegation and members of the embassy staff who would be working with us, marking the beginning of a close working relationship between the delegation and the embassy. Notwithstanding the constraints imposed by limited staffing and the cramped and inadequate offices from which they operated, Ambassador Polansky and his staff were unstinting in providing both administrative and substantive support to our delegation. The delegation was comfortably installed in the Sheraton Sofia Hotel Balkan, a first-class international hotel located in the heart of the historic Bulgarian capital. I was fascinated to see that immediately behind our hotel was an active archaeological dig uncovering an extensive Roman ruin. The meeting itself was held in a newly built, spacious, and attractive conference center.

I was pleased on arriving in Sofia to find that Turkey had made a last-minute decision to attend the meeting and would be represented by officials from its embassy in Sofia. Apparently, our arguments in favor of Turkey's attendance had in the end been effective. In their opening statements at the meeting, Turkey, the United States, and virtually all Western delegations made reference to Bulgaria's repression of its ethnic Turks. These statements took up much of the first week of the meeting.

Turkey's presence made a critical difference and ensured a high degree of Western unity in vigorously addressing human rights issues. Also, the government of Bulgaria, eager to take the edge off the harsh criticism aimed at it, showed remarkable tolerance toward dissident Bulgarian environmental groups. Further, in a noteworthy conciliatory gesture, Bulgaria agreed to meet with Turkey on October 30 in a neutral location (Kuwait) to discuss the issues raised regarding Bulgaria's ethnic Turkish minority.

Before the conference began and during its early stages, Gilder, deputy head of the U.S. delegation, visited Turkey and outlying areas in Bulgaria and was able to confirm that serious human rights abuses were being inflicted on ethnic Turks in Bulgaria. In public statements and press conferences, he took the lead in denouncing those abuses and providing specific information on individuals who had been targeted by the Bulgarian government. Bulgarian Foreign Minister Petar Mladenov expressed his displeasure with Gilder's activities to Ambassador Polansky.

Mladenov stopped short of pursuing his case against Gilder and seeking redress, presumably to avoid inflaming the issue any further on the threshold of the CSCE meeting. Within the Bulgarian government, Mladenov had been a strong advocate of holding this meeting in Sofia as a means of improving Bulgaria's image internationally. (Bulgaria at the time had a well-earned reputation as a doctrinaire and subservient satellite of the Soviet Union.)

On the evening of October 17, members of the Bulgarian environmental NGO Ecoglasnost[2] held a press conference in an apartment in central Sofia. They discussed the specifics of the CSCE meeting's environmental agenda and noted that one of Ecoglasnost's members, Dr. Petar Beron, a leading zoologist, was an adviser on the Bulgarian delegation to the CSCE meeting. They also talked about prior harassment of their group by local security forces and ridiculed a lower court decision denying Ecoglasnost's application for official registration.

This dramatic event in a crowded apartment was the first public press conference by an independent group in Bulgaria in more than 40 years. Ecoglasnost capitalized on the opportunity by inviting foreign journalists who were in town for the CSCE meeting. Gilder and I attended along with others from our delegation, as well as officials from the U.S. embassy and several other

Western embassies. The police and security forces that milled about in the street outside the apartment house had never seen anything like it and seemed puzzled and confused by it all.

Ecoglasnost was openly seeking international support for its environmental goals. Alexander Karakachanov, its executive secretary, stated, "There is no turning back." Ecoglasnost was conducting its own analysis of environmental threats, and it used this occasion to announce that it would be inviting the public to a program on its findings at a local hall.

Following a statement he made to the CSCE meeting on October 19, Gilder and I held a press conference that was attended by more than 50 media representatives and a number of Bulgarian human rights activists. Gilder gave a balanced assessment of the Bulgarian human rights scene. He noted that recent decisions by the Bulgarian government, reflected in a new passport law, would make it easier to reunite families divided by migration. He welcomed a decision by a committee of the National Assembly to ease restrictions on freedom of religion and on speaking languages other than Bulgarian. Gilder referred favorably to the fact that the government of Bulgaria had not prevented human rights activists from attending the CSCE conference and had included a member of Ecoglasnost as an adviser on the Bulgarian delegation. At the same time, he made clear that continuing harsh treatment of the Turkish ethnic minority and human rights activists would not be ignored.

In his speech to the delegates to the meeting earlier that day, Gilder had named four Bulgarian activists as "brave crusaders for human rights": Anton Zaprianov, Koyana Trencheva, Georgi Spassov, and Slavomir Tsankov. He deplored the harassment and detention that they had suffered at the hands of the Bulgarian government. All four of them attended our press conference as guests of the U.S. delegation, and each of them made comments and referred to the hardship and abuse that they had encountered. Thus, this press conference provided another platform for the small group of Bulgarian human rights activists who used the CSCE environmental meeting as an unprecedented opportunity to express their views.

Trencheva described how her husband and five other activists had been detained for more than three months, even though no indictment had been issued against them. Gilder denounced the actions taken against the activists and termed them violations of rights that were guaranteed under CSCE. He noted that in the Trencheva case, the United States had already formally invoked procedures under CSCE to object to Bulgaria's actions.

From the first days of the meeting, I joined other delegates from the Western countries to form a NATO caucus that met to coordinate views and consult on proposals being considered for presentation to the conference. These caucus sessions, which took place frequently—sometimes more than once a day—proved critical in keeping us working closely together and responding effectively to events as they occurred.

In a meeting of the NATO heads of delegation on October 23, the French delegation raised a troublesome issue by saying that it intended to have a proposal on industrial accidents presented to the meeting, sponsored by "France/European Community." We had agreed before the meeting that France, which was serving its term as the president of the European Community (EC), could use that designation on its nameplate. However, I took the position, joined by other non-EC delegations, that the EC was not itself a CSCE participating state, and any formal recognition of it, such as listing it as the sponsor of a proposal, was unacceptable.

The immediate problem was resolved when France agreed to reformulate its proposal and present it to the meeting as a "nonpaper," which would not require official sponsorship. This question regarding the role of the EC, however, remained a somewhat contentious background issue within the NATO caucus.

The first week of the meeting was quite successful (as measured against U.S. objectives). In addition to the attention given to human rights issues, well-thought-out proposals on the environmental agenda were put forward, drawing on the expertise of environmental specialists attending the meeting as delegation members. EPA officials on the U.S. delegation made several presentations; one briefing, presented by senior EPA official John Gustafson, concerned EPA's community outreach program, which is designed to keep the public informed about environmental issues that might affect them.

The Eastern bloc countries welcomed the input of the environmental experts, and the negotiations on environmental issues went smoothly. In this positive atmosphere, a broad push was developing for a final consensus document at the end of the meeting.

On October 25, U.S. Ambassador Polansky hosted a reception at his residence for leading Bulgarian dissidents. This was the first such gathering hosted by the embassy. Western press representatives and members of the U.S. delegation also attended the reception. The relaxed atmosphere stimulated an extraordinary interchange between the dissidents and the other guests, which led to such tangible results as planned academic exchanges and on-the-record interviews with Western reporters.

Environmentalists under Attack

On Thursday morning, October 26, the unprecedented official tolerance toward Ecoglasnost activists came to a sharp and brutal end. A group of black-jacketed men—plainclothes state security operatives—pounced on nine Ecoglasnost leaders who were on their way to a park in central Sofia. They were roughly herded into a bus and taken to another park in the southern outskirts of the city. In the process, some were kicked and beaten. Subsequently, uniformed militia detained or transported by bus to the outskirts another 15 to 20 Ecoglasnost members who were at the central Sofia park. They had been gathering to collect signatures for a petition related to an environmental issue. These events were witnessed by members of the delegations of Canada, France, the United Kingdom, and the United States, as well as reporters from the BBC, Radio Free Europe, and an Egyptian news service.

At the afternoon session of the CSCE meeting, the Bulgarian authorities were widely and harshly criticized by Western delegations, who demanded a full explanation of what had happened before the work of the meeting could continue. I made clear that the United States would need assurances that no such abuses would occur again before we would be willing to continue to take part in the meeting. I had called for an emergency meeting of the NATO caucus earlier that day and had confirmed that all the NATO delegations shared that position.

The next day, Friday morning, Bulgarian Environment Minister Nikolay Dyulgerov took the chair for the Bulgarian delegation. He expressed regret for the events of the previous day and conceded that the authorities in this instance had been "tactless" and had exceeded their proper bounds. He said that orders had been issued to ensure that Bulgaria would meet its CSCE responsibilities both inside and outside the meeting hall, adding that he hoped we could now proceed in the constructive spirit that had previously been established. It was as clear and unequivocal an apology as one is ever likely to hear from a government official. Nonetheless, Dyulgerov could not resist suggesting that there had been provocation and implying that the press and some delegations had been behaving in ways that abused the hospitality extended by Bulgaria.

Following an extended break, the session reconvened to hear delegation after delegation welcome Bulgaria's expression of regret and assurances for the future, while rejecting references to provocation and improper behavior by delegation members and the press. I was particularly struck by the critical comments Bulgaria received from its putative allies: Hungary, Poland, and the Soviet Union.

In my presentation, I emphasized that it was not enough to be sensitive to CSCE undertakings only while the Sofia meeting was in progress. CSCE-guaranteed rights were not "three-week rights," but permanent ones. I said that on the basis of eyewitness reports, it was clear that the provocation in the previous day's events did not come from the side of the environmentalists or from delegation members or the press. I also expressed concern that substantive CSCE rights not be undermined by administrative measures, such as last-minute shifts in permitted locations for assemblies, as appeared to have occurred in this instance.

At the end of the morning session, in an atmosphere that hardly could have been more propitious, I introduced a U.S.

proposal on the right of the public to be informed about environmental issues and the right of environmental NGOs to make their views known and to be listened to by their governments. I said that I would be making a fuller presentation on our proposal on the following Monday. This kept the issue alive and gave us some time to observe the implementation of the Bulgarian assurances and to work on maximizing the number of cosponsors of our resolution.

Concluding on an Upbeat Note

Notwithstanding the traumatic incident involving Ecoglasnost, we were ending the week's roller-coaster ride at a high point. It now appeared that the meeting was headed toward a successful conclusion and that a consensus on a final document might be possible. Delegations representing the neutral countries—Austria, Finland, Sweden, and Switzerland—were completing work on draft proposals dealing with the environmental agenda items suitable for inclusion in a final document. The U.S. proposal dealing with public awareness and the rights of environmental NGOs appeared likely to gain wide acceptance.

There were, however, clouds on the horizon. Romania, which was still headed by the repressive Communist dictator Nicolae Ceauşescu, might balk at accepting the broad rights given to environmental NGOs under the U.S. proposal. And Turkey, although pleased with how the meeting was going, might not accept a final document that did not make specific reference to the ethnic Turkish minority issue, a point on which, given inevitable Bulgarian opposition, consensus would surely be unobtainable.

After Bulgaria's expression of regret and assurances for the future, the reestablished positive attitude in the meeting was sustained through its final session on November 3, 1989. A final document was prepared that included the U.S. proposed language on public awareness and the rights of NGOs, as well as language on each of the environmental issues on the agenda. These elements had been worked out in the NATO caucus, based on the drafts prepared by the four neutral delegations. Turkey agreed to join the consensus on the final document, even though it did not contain a reference to the Turkish ethnic minority in Bulgaria. As feared, however, Romania refused to go along with the language on the rights of environmental NGOs, blocking a consensus on the final document.

Attempts to persuade Romania to join the consensus were fruitless, leaving the other 34 delegations frustrated and angry. In the course of a meeting of the NATO caucus, an idea emerged for a way around the problem that had not been used before in a CSCE meeting: we could convert the final document into a proposal cosponsored by 34 of the 35 CSCE delegations. This innovative approach would leave a clear record of how broadly the draft final document had been supported and how completely isolated Romania was in opposing it.

Other delegations agreed to this approach and, in lieu of a consensus final document, the broadly sponsored proposal was the final result of the meeting. (Interestingly, it was a rare instance of agreement on any proposal by the unlikely trio of Bulgaria, Turkey, and Greece.) Because of CSCE's consensus decisionmaking principle, the meeting ended with no agreed final document, but the proposal for a final document, supported by all but one delegation, put on record what such a document would have said, but for the opposition of Romania.

A Sofia Assessment

Although there was initially a great deal of concern and uncertainty regarding the prospects for this meeting, we were in the end remarkably successful in achieving the full range of U.S. objectives. Despite Romania's blocking of a final consensus document, we succeeded in demonstrating the commitment of the other 34 CSCE countries to a high standard of rights for environmentalists and their organizations.

We also developed sound and constructive texts on the three environmental topics on the agenda—transboundary effects of industrial accidents, transboundary waterways, and hazardous chemicals. These were also included in the broadly sponsored proposal for a final document.

Importantly, the environmental proposals built on work already under way in such well-respected forums as the United Nations Economic Commission for Europe and the OECD. For example, the proposed final document called for the UN's commission to develop an international agreement on the prevention and control of the transboundary effects of industrial accidents. The proposals also provided for closer coordination among the CSCE countries on environmental issues.

The language on the rights of environmentalists in the proposed final document, on which Romania alone blocked a consensus, was strong and unequivocal. The participating states, with the exception of Romania, affirmed their respect for the right of individuals, groups, and organizations concerned with environmental issues to express freely their views, to associate with others, to peacefully assemble, as well as to obtain, publish, and distribute information on these issues, without legal and administrative impediments inconsistent with the CSCE provisions. They asserted that these individuals, groups, and organizations have the right to participate in public debates on environmental issues, as well as to establish and maintain direct and independent contacts at the national and international levels.

The creative way in which we turned a draft final document on which consensus could not be achieved into a proposal cosponsored by 34 of the 35 delegations had some distinct advantages. The 34 sponsoring states became even more closely associated with the undertakings in the proposal than if they had more passively joined a consensus in favor of them. Further, this procedure sharply and visibly isolated Romania, putting it clearly outside the CSCE mainstream in recognizing the rights of environmentalists. This was a much healthier result for the CSCE process than having Romania join a consensus, but try to duck certain commitments through an interpretive statement (as it had sought to do in a CSCE meeting earlier that year in Vienna).

Events taking place in Bulgaria provided a historic context for the meeting. We and other delegations were clearly influencing the course of those events through the positions that we were taking. For example, after we threatened to leave the meeting following the abuse of Ecoglasnost demonstrators, Bulgaria made and followed through on assurances that it would not mistreat dissidents. After that incident, the Bulgarian authorities showed increasing tolerance of the activities of environmentalists, whose demonstrations grew to thousands of participants. Comparable demonstrations had not taken place in Bulgaria since the immediate post–World War II period.

Shortly after the conference ended, Bulgaria's hard-line leader Zhivkov, who had been in power for 35 years, was replaced by the moderate foreign minister, Petar Mladenov. This signaled the coming end of that country's era as a Communist satellite of the USSR. Mladenov was a reformer in the mold of Gorbachev and Shevardnadze and reportedly was privately encouraged by those Soviet leaders in his confrontation with Zhivkov.

Zhivkov had become increasingly anxious and concerned by the press conferences and assemblies stimulated by the CSCE meeting. He feared—for good reason, as it turned out—that his authority was being undermined. Soon after the meeting, Zhivkov lost his leadership position and was jailed for acts committed during the Communist era, such as the harassment and imprisonment of dissidents. A number of Ecoglasnost leaders had prominent roles in subsequent Bulgarian governments. The Sofia meeting thus advanced in a very direct way the fundamental CSCE objective of the Western democracies of promoting political reform in the Eastern bloc.

Obviously, what was happening in Bulgaria was part of the general breakup of the USSR and its satellite system. The Berlin Wall fell on November 9, 1989, just after the end of the CSCE meeting in Sofia. However, the Sofia meeting apparently did help speed up the process of political change in Bulgaria. Perhaps the change in Bulgaria took place with less violence and disruption than would have been the case if the meeting had not taken place. Bulgaria did not experience the chaos and bloodshed that characterized the transition from communism in neighboring Romania. Secretary of State James Baker cited the impact of the meeting several months later in a speech he gave to the National Governors Association:

> It was an international environmental conference in Sofia, Bulgaria, which helped to spark the popular revolution. The "Ecoglasnost Association," formed in anticipation of that meeting, is now one of Bulgaria's largest grassroots organizations and democratic opposition groups. So in Bulgaria, Ecoglasnost gave "green revolution" a whole new meaning.[3]

We did several things right in this effort. Our decisions to attend this meeting, to press Bulgaria hard on its human rights record and its treatment of its ethnic Turkish minority, and to urge Turkey to attend all proved sound. At the time we made those decisions, it was not a sure thing that such a strategy would pay off. It might have elicited a much more hostile reaction from Bulgaria and resulted in a failed CSCE meeting in Sofia.

Turkey's last-minute decision to be represented at the meeting was crucial to the success we were able to achieve. Turkey's presence protected the integrity of the CSCE process and also helped in bringing all the Western countries together in condemning Bulgaria's repression of its Turkish minority. More generally, it helped keep human rights issues a central concern of the meeting. Bulgaria reacted positively, easing its mistreatment of dissidents and the Turkish minority and agreeing for the first time to meet with Turkey to address their binational problem.

Our use of NATO groupings as coordinating mechanisms proved extremely effective, both before and during the Sofia meeting. The NATO caucus in Sofia was the means by which we were able to rapidly develop and sustain common positions and strategies in the face of fast-breaking developments. At key junctures, the NATO caucus met as often as two or three times a day.

In sum, working closely with other delegations, the United States was able to contribute to the result in Sofia that was both good for the CSCE process and constructive in advancing the particular environmental issues addressed. Importantly, the principle that human rights issues were always in order at a CSCE meeting, whatever else was on the agenda, was upheld and confirmed.

chapter 8

Fishing in the Donut Hole

B y the end of the 1970s, nearly every country with a coastline had declared a 200-mile exclusive economic zone within which it controlled marine resources. These EEZs were sanctioned by the draft United Nations Convention on the Law of the Sea, which was then under negotiation. The outer limits of the U.S. and the USSR EEZs enclosed a roughly round area within the Aleutian Basin in the central Bering Sea. This enclosed pocket of high seas—outside the reach of any country's EEZ—had come to be called the "Bering Sea Donut Hole."[1]

The Bering Sea was richly endowed with fisheries resources, notably pollock. During the 1970s, as the world's cod and haddock stocks were being depleted, pollock became an increasingly popular food. This led to greater fishing effort, beginning in the late 1970s, directed at the abundant pollock stocks in the Bering Sea. There was an especially strong and growing demand in Japan, where pollock was used for making surimi, a minced substance processed to resemble expensive shellfish products, such as crab legs, scallops, and shrimp.

In 1977, lacking a significant pollock fleet of its own, the United States began allocating, for a fee, surplus pollock in its EEZ in the Bering Sea to other fishing nations. The USSR did the same. Both countries then proceeded to develop trawling fleets of their own

The Bering Sea, showing the Donut Hole (1993).

—U.S. Department of State,
Office of the Geographer and Global Issues

capable of exploiting the pollock stocks in their respective EEZs, which together constitute about 90 percent of the Bering Sea. The Donut Hole in the center consists of some 50,000 square miles of international waters.

As the USSR and the United States expanded their capacities to catch pollock, they began phasing out their EEZ allocations of these fish to countries with distant-water fishing fleets. By the end of the 1970s, the U.S. pollock fishing fleet was harvesting product with a retail value of some $2 billion annually. In Alaska, Oregon, and Washington, some 20,000 people were engaged in catching and processing pollock.[2] The United States no longer had any surplus pollock to allocate to foreign countries, and the USSR was sharply reducing allocations in its EEZ.

To compensate for the lost fishing opportunities in the Soviet and U.S. EEZs, the distant-water fishing fleets of Japan and the

Republic of Korea (South Korea) turned their attention to fishing for pollock in the Donut Hole. Even though the Donut Hole was a less attractive pollock fishery than that provided by the shallower waters of the EEZs, by 1985 long-range fishing fleets from China and Poland had joined them. These fleets consisted of large, high-capacity factory trawlers.

This intense concentration of fishing led to a significant degra-dation of the pollock stock in the Donut Hole. Because pollock moved between the Donut Hole and the Soviet and U.S. EEZs, fishing in those zones was also negatively affected. Also, vessels in the Donut Hole sometimes crossed into the Soviet and U.S. EEZs and fished illegally. The U.S. fishery was particularly affected. Fisheries scientists believed that the pollock stock in the Donut Hole spawned near Bogoslof Island in the U.S. EEZ.

On March 21, 1988, the U.S. Senate passed a resolution on the need to stop uncontrolled fishing in the international waters of the Bering Sea. In that same year, scientists from the six nations participating in the fishery met in Sitka, Alaska, to discuss the state of the pollock resource. Their findings suggested that inter-national cooperation in managing the fishery was needed, but the countries concerned did not take any follow-up action.

By the time of the U.S.-USSR summit meeting held in Wash-ington in June 1990, the situation in the central Bering Sea had become sufficiently alarming that President George H. W. Bush and Soviet leader Mikhail Gorbachev called for urgent conser-vation measures to be taken. They noted that international law, as codified in the 1982 Law of the Sea Convention, provided for coastal states and distant-water fishing states to cooperate in ensuring the conservation of living marine resources in the high seas.[3] Even though the United States had not ratified the conven-tion, both Democratic and Republican administrations made it clear that they supported its provisions.

Seeking a Cooperative Solution

At the end of 1990, the United States, in coordination with the USSR, invited China, Japan, Poland, and South Korea to a conference to consider arrangements for the conservation of the living marine resources in the Bering Sea Donut Hole. This meeting, which would be the first in a series of 10 such conferences over a period of three years, took place in Washington in February 1991. The U.S. negotiating effort was led throughout by David Colson, who had recently been appointed deputy assistant secretary for oceans and fisheries in the State Department's Bureau of Oceans and International Environmental and Scientific Affairs.

At the initial conference, agreement was reached to freeze the pollock catch at the 1985 level.[4] The conference also agreed to discourage other countries from fishing in the Donut Hole, to standardize catch reporting, and to accelerate scientific research on the fishery.

The second conference was held in Tokyo from July 31 to August 2, 1991. That conference was presented with data showing that the pollock stock in the central Bering Sea had declined to a point where pollock fishing could no longer be supported, even at the 1985 catch level. Nonetheless, the distant-water fishing states, sensitive to the economic and political importance of their domestic fishing interests, rejected a call by the USSR and the United States for a moratorium on fishing in the Donut Hole. The conference participants also failed to reach agreement on proposed interim measures, such as the deployment of onboard scientific observers and the use of satellite location transmitters on the fishing vessels, which would permit all the concerned countries to be aware of the location of vessels fishing in the Donut Hole.

The United States presented to the conference a proposal for an international convention that would address the conservation and management needs of the resources of the Donut Hole over the long term.[5] It was rejected by the distant-water fishing states as being one-sided in favor of the coastal states, giving those states too dominant a role in the management of the fishery. The delegates to the conference agreed to meet again in Washington in November 1991 to continue discussions of both urgent interim measures and long-term management measures.

At the November conference in Washington, the delegates confronted the fact that the pollock catch in the Donut Hole had declined from a peak of 1.4 million metric tons in 1989 to 260,000 metric tons at the end of the third quarter of 1991. Despite this and other evidence that the pollock stock was collapsing, the distant-water fishing countries continued to oppose a moratorium on fishing in the Donut Hole. They agreed, however, that catch levels should be substantially reduced in 1992. They also now agreed to the deployment of onboard observers and to the use of location transmitters on fishing vessels during the 1992 fishing season.

The United States was deeply disappointed with the slow rate of progress. In a series of further conferences, the U.S. delegation continued to press both for more action in addressing the current urgent problem of a collapsing pollock stock and for the negotiation of a convention that would deal with long-term issues. It was a difficult undertaking because we were seeking to break new ground in the multilateral management of a fishery in international waters.

The UN Convention on the Law of the Sea, though it called for cooperation between coastal and distant-water fishing states in conserving high-seas fisheries resources, gave no guidance as to how this would be accomplished. While accepting that they had a responsibility to cooperate in the conservation of marine resources, the distant-water fishing countries cited the right of all nations to fish on the high seas, and they were still reluctant to accept any significant restrictions on their vessels in the Donut Hole.

Progress at the next conference, in Tokyo, continued to be painfully slow, but at the fifth conference, in Moscow in August 1992, the parties finally agreed to a suspension of fishing in the Donut Hole in 1993 and 1994. The total catch of pollock in the area during the first six months of 1992 had been less than 11,000 metric tons. At that catch level, it did not make economic sense to continue to send distant-water fishing fleets to the central Bering Sea. The Russian Federation (the USSR dissolved in December 1991)[6] and the United States also suspended fishing for pollock in their own EEZs.

By the eighth conference, in Seoul in October 1993, the participants had reached or were close to agreement on certain elements of a convention that would govern the pollock fishery in the Donut Hole. But significant differences remained over some central provisions. These included, for example, how the allowable harvest levels would be established once the pollock stocks had recovered and how individual country quotas would be set. All agreed on the gravity of the situation and on the need to conclude the negotiation of a draft convention by the end of 1993. With this goal in mind, the delegates agreed to meet again, for the ninth time, in Washington from November 29 to December 3, 1993.

The Critical Ninth Conference

The host country is normally expected to provide the chair for an international conference. If Colson were to take on that task, his ability to play his critical role as leader of the U.S. delegation would be constrained. He would need, for example, to sustain support within the U.S. delegation for the compromises that would be required to reach agreement on the text of a convention. He therefore asked for my help with the ninth conference. If I chaired the conference, he would be free to devote his full time and attention to leading the U.S. delegation during this critical stage of the negotiation. I agreed to do so.

The conference's opening session took place in the State Department's Loy Henderson Conference Room, a large and impressive UN-style meeting space. After welcoming the delegates to Washington, I said that their first job was to select a chairperson for the meeting. I opened the floor for nominations. As Colson had arranged with his fellow heads of delegation, I was the only one nominated and was voted in by acclamation. This was followed by a round of brief opening statements by representatives of each of the countries at the meeting.

Feeling that no real progress could be made in such a formal plenary session, I quickly ended this opening meeting. After eight such conferences, there was no point in having the delegations sit around listening to each other restate and elaborate on their positions. At my suggestion, we adjourned to a less formal meeting room where I chaired a "working group of the whole." In that setting, sitting around a table together, the delegations could speak more openly and explore the compromises that would have to be made if we were to reach an agreement. The core issues that we faced could be readily stated. How would the concerned countries reach agreement on the state of the pollock stocks and set an allowable total harvest level? Once that was done, how would the allowable catch be divided among those countries? An important subsidiary issue concerned monitoring and enforcing any agreed fishing limitations. Another sensitive issue involved the balance between pollock fisheries in the Donut Hole and the adjacent EEZs of the coastal states, Russia and the United States. The perspectives of the distant-water fishing states and the coastal states differed; however, all shared a strong interest in the recovery of the Bering Sea pollock stock and the reestablishment of a viable fishery in which all the countries could participate.

Agreement did not come easily, but we did achieve breakthroughs on the major issues. I found it helpful in several instances to interrupt our working group meetings to consult with only the heads of delegation on how we could break apparent deadlocks in the negotiation. We gathered on the overstuffed couch and chairs in the OES assistant secretary's office and engaged in a freewheeling search for possible areas of compromise.

As anticipated, one of the most difficult matters to resolve was how we would decide substantive issues, such as the level of the pollock biomass (the total tonnage of pollock in the fishery). Russia and the United States, as the coastal states, sought a veto over such substantive decisions, but that was unacceptable to the other countries. The distant-water states made two alternative proposals for a decisionmaking principle: majority vote or consensus.

As chair, I asserted that both those decisionmaking proposals were unworkable. They were formulas that were destined to lead to an impasse. Under the "majority rules" approach, the coastal states could be outvoted, a situation that they would not tolerate. The principle of consensus meant that any one country could block needed decisions. I undertook to consult with the heads of delegation to seek a way to resolve this problem.

Drawing on those consultations, and especially on my close working relationship with Colson and the U.S. delegation, I came back to a working group meeting of the delegations with a "chairman's proposal." It provided for a phased decisionmaking procedure and contained the following elements:

(1) Nonsubstantive decisions (generally considered to be routine procedural matters) would be taken by majority vote at the annual conference to be held under the convention.

(2) Substantive decisions would be taken by consensus at the annual conference. Any party to the convention could designate any decision as substantive.

(3) On the critical substantive issues—the determination of the total pollock biomass in the Aleutian Basin and the allowable harvest level in the Donut Hole—a fallback procedure for reaching decisions would be contained in an annex to be used "if every effort to achieve consensus has failed." In such instances, institutions designated by Russia and the United States, as the coastal states of the Bering Sea, would jointly determine the pollock biomass level, based on information reviewed by the scientific and technical committee. (This committee would be set up under the convention and would include representatives from each of the parties to the convention.)

(4) If the institutions designated by Russia and the United States were unable to jointly determine a total pollock biomass level for the Aleutian Basin, then the level would be set in relation to the size of the pollock biomass determined by the United States to exist in the area off Bogoslof Island in the U.S. EEZ—a known spawning area for the Aleutian Basin pollock stock. On the basis of experience in previous years, the Bogoslof Island biomass would be deemed to be 60 percent of the total biomass in the Aleutian Basin.

(5) Once the total pollock biomass in the Aleutian Basin had been determined, if the annual conference was unable to reach a consensus on the allowable harvest level, the allowable harvest for the Donut Hole would be set in accordance with the following schedule:

Pollock biomass	Allowable harvest level
Less than 1.67 million metric tons	Moratorium on fishing
1.67 to 2.00 million metric tons	130,000 metric tons
2.00 to 2.5 million metric tons	190,000 metric tons
2.5 million metric tons or more	To be determined by consensus

The difficult question of how the total allowable harvest level would be divided among the parties was also addressed in the proposal. If, once that level had been set, the annual conference could not reach a consensus on individual national quotas, another provision in the annex to the convention would become operative. That provision would call on the parties to set an opening date for the pollock fishery in the convention area. The catch of all the countries participating in the fishery would then be continuously monitored, and when the total allowable catch level was reached, the fishery would be immediately closed.

The chairman's proposal, although it may have had the appearance of Rube Goldberg–style expediency, provided a basis for agreement among all the participating countries. All were prepared to accept the inherent uncertainties in this decision-making procedure, thus overcoming the last significant barrier to successfully concluding the negotiation. The procedure gave assurance that once the pollock stock had recovered sufficiently, we would be able to make the decisions necessary to restart a sustainable fishery in the Donut Hole.

The delegates recognized that the lack of advance agreement on allowable harvest levels corresponding to biomass levels over 2.5 million metric tons was a loose end, but a rebuilding of the pollock stock to those levels seemed so remote that the participating countries were willing to live with it. Significantly, the proposal confirmed that the existing moratorium on fishing in the Donut Hole would continue as long as the pollock biomass was less than 1.67 million metric tons.

The biomass formulation also implied a link to what would be happening in the U.S. EEZ. The United States had been in the practice of closing the Bogoslof Island pollock fishery in its EEZ whenever the pollock biomass there fell to 1 million metric tons, which was 60 percent of the 1.67 million metric ton level that would trigger the closing of the pollock fishery in the Donut Hole. Thus, one could anticipate that when the fishery was closed in the Donut Hole, it would also be closed in the U.S. EEZ. This addressed an important issue of equity between coastal and distant-water fishing states in the sacrifices that would be made to conserve the stock.

We were also making good progress on monitoring and enforcement issues. The delegates confirmed earlier indications that their countries were, as part of the convention provisions, prepared to accept scientific observers from other parties to the convention on all vessels fishing in the Donut Hole. We also tied down the understanding that all vessels in the fishery would be equipped with satellite position-fixing devices. This was of special importance to the United States, which was concerned that distant-water fishing vessels in the Donut Hole would enter the U.S. EEZ. Further, we reached agreement that all parties would receive 48 hours' advance notice of any fishing vessel that would be entering the Donut Hole.

A major breakthrough was acceptance of the principle that fisheries enforcement officials from any of the parties to the convention could board the fishing vessels of any of the other parties to monitor compliance with the convention's provisions. Such high-seas boardings previously had been permitted only on the basis of advance permission granted in each instance by the flag state of the fishing vessel (the state in whose territory the vessel is registered). For the first time, we were contemplating including blanket permission for such boardings in international waters as part of a multilateral fisheries agreement. This was particularly significant because nearly all the enforcement vessels patrolling the Donut Hole would be from the coastal states, mostly from the United States.

The conference had reached a point where we had at least tentative agreement on all the essential issues. However, the delegates to the conference were not quite ready to declare the project completed. Delegates had achieved compromises by moving from some long-held positions, so they wanted an opportunity to review the proposals with their governments at home.

The participating countries agreed to meet again as soon as possible to complete a draft of the agreement. For that purpose, another meeting was scheduled to be held February 7–11, 1994, in Washington.

The Final Conference

I was scheduled to retire from the Foreign Service in January 1994. Colson and OES Assistant Secretary Elinor Constable were concerned that if I could not chair the tenth conference, we would risk losing the momentum that we had achieved in the meeting just concluded. Some of the major understandings that we had reached in that ninth round were quite fragile and had been put together based on my interventions as chair. I agreed to stay on to chair the final conference if the Foreign Service could be persuaded to adjust my scheduled retirement date.

Constable wrote to the director general of the Foreign Service urging the unusual step of extending my mandatory retirement date so that I could chair the upcoming conference. She wrote, "Our success at that meeting will largely relate to the chair's success in moving the proceedings along, and using good offices to broker or suggest compromises." She noted that I had gained the confidence of the country delegations, all of whom had asked that I chair the final conference. The director general agreed that my retirement date could be changed to the day after the conclusion of the next conference.

At the February conference, the understandings that we had previously reached held firm. The outlines of an agreement were in place, and we turned to the painstaking task of completing a draft convention that all the heads of delegation could initial. There were still details to be worked out: for example, although it was agreed that onboard scientific observers would be accepted, we needed to agree on who would pay for them. In that instance, the basic compromise was that the fishing vessels would absorb the cost of maintaining the observers on board, while the country that sent them would meet the cost of their training and transportation to the vessel.

The conference participants also agreed to a "record of discussions" to deal with certain matters not covered in the draft convention or its annex. In addition to addressing some technical matters, it included language on the delicate issue of the relationship between pollock fishing in the Donut Hole and that in the EEZs of Russia and the United States. The distant-water fishing states did not want to control fishing for pollock in the Donut Hole unless pollock fishing in the adjacent EEZs was similarly limited. The delegates agreed in the record of discussions that the management of pollock fishing in the Donut Hole and the adjacent EEZs should be compatible and consistent.

Russia and the United States wanted the convention to go beyond pollock and include a commitment to deal cooperatively with other marine resource issues that might arise in the Donut Hole. The other countries, however, were not prepared to go that far. As a compromise, the delegates agreed that the science and technical committee to be established under the convention could look at other resource issues and report its findings to the annual conference. The parties would have to agree by consensus before any such nonpollock resource issues could be considered further.

On February 10, we were finally ready to prepare a draft convention acceptable to all the participants. The United States, which was providing staffing services for the conference, undertook to prepare the draft overnight. We scheduled a final session for the next day, Friday, February 11, at which the heads of delegation would initial the convention, signaling their agreement to recommend it to their governments for signature.

We encountered one last obstacle: the weather forecast for Friday called for one of Washington's rare blizzards. The U.S. government announced that federal agencies in the Washington area would be closed for the day.

All the delegations agreed that we could not let another conference end without initialing an agreed draft. Since many delegates had commitments that would prevent them from staying in Washington beyond February 11, we all decided to show up at the State Department for the initialing ceremony, snow or no snow. OES had to make special arrangements quickly, including arranging for guards, who would otherwise have had the day off, to open the State Department for this purpose.

On that snowy Friday, all the delegations made it to the Loy Henderson Conference Room, where the first meeting of this conference had been held three years earlier, for one last plenary session. The mood was jubilant, even though some delegates had just trudged from their hotels through nearly two feet of snow. After the initialing of the convention, the head of the Russian delegation, V. K. Zilanov, on behalf of the assembled delegates, presented me with a blue T-shirt imprinted with a map of the Donut Hole and the surrounding area, with the caption "Smith of the Bering Sea."

A Precedent-Setting Agreement

The United States, as the depository country for the agreement, opened the Convention on the Conservation and Management of Pollock Resources in the Central Bering Sea for signature on June 4, 1994. The convention was soon signed and ratified by all the participating countries. In his signing statement on June 16, 1994, Dave Colson said that with the conclusion of the convention "... we stand on the brink of a new era in fisheries conservation and management."

Indeed, we had successfully negotiated a comprehensive multilateral agreement for managing a fishery in international waters. It included a precedent-setting decisionmaking regime to ensure that necessary decisions could be made even in the absence of a consensus among the parties to the agreement. Further, it broke new ground by incorporating blanket permission for enforcement officials of any of the participating countries to board at any time the vessels of other parties operating in the Donut Hole to monitor compliance with the convention.

Although a regional agreement, the convention had global implications. It came at a time when, in UN forums and elsewhere, countries were exploring the operational meaning of the Law of the Sea Convention's call for cooperation between distant-water fishing states and coastal states to conserve marine resources in the high seas. The Donut Hole agreement put flesh on the bare bones of the Law of the Sea Convention's language.[7]

The Path to an Accord

How was it possible to achieve this positive result? Dogged determination and persistence on the part of all concerned over a three-year negotiation is part of the answer. Also, the arrangements for the critical final two conferences played an important role. With Dave Colson free to be a full-time head of delegation for the United States and my playing the part of an active, compromise-seeking chair, we were able to break out of the impasses that had been encountered over the course of the negotiation.

Procedurally, I believe that getting quickly out of plenary session, thus avoiding repetitive and often confrontational statements of national positions, contributed greatly to the progress made in the ninth conference. In the informal working group, and particularly in the small sessions that I held with the heads of delegation, we were able to address the hard decisions and consider the compromises necessary to resolve them. In those meetings, we were largely able to put aside the concept that we were in a contest to protect and advance our competing national interests. Rather, we created the sense that we were working together to find a way to address the hard reality of a collapsed pollock fishery and the interest that we all shared in its recovery.

There were other factors that helped account for the success of the negotiation. The talks had been initiated by two of the world's major powers, the United States and the USSR. The other countries had to take the exercise seriously. They were aware that if the attempt to achieve multilateral cooperation failed, those two countries might well take action themselves to exclude distant-water fishing fleets from the Bering Sea Donut Hole.

Finally, it was significant that since the fifth conference, in August 1992, all the participating countries had voluntarily suspended their pollock fisheries in the Donut Hole, given the collapse of the stock. It was no doubt easier for them to agree to measures that would affect a renewed pollock fishery in the future than to negotiate shares of an existing fishery. By the end of the negotiation, the distant-water fishing states were no longer being asked to trade away current benefits to achieve an agreement that would regulate uncertain future fishing opportunities.

Despite the moratorium on fishing there, the pollock stock in the Donut Hole remains in poor shape. The stock has not yet recovered to the point where renewed fishing can be contemplated, and it is uncertain when it will do so. The pollock biomass is being assessed and monitored regularly by the science and technical committee, which reports to the annual conference of the parties to the convention.

When the pollock stock recovers sufficiently, the machinery will be in place to renew the fishery on a sustainable basis. This agreement has set an important precedent in showing how coastal states and distant-water fishing states can cooperate in managing fisheries in international waters in which they share an interest.

chapter 9

On Finding
Common Ground

The eight negotiations recounted in this book show the potential of diplomacy as a tool for dealing with environmental and scientific challenges faced by the world community. Even when national interests differed sharply, common ground could be found to serve as a basis for mutually beneficial agreements.

The decade between the mid-1980s and the mid-1990s was notable not only for an increase in the number of environment and science negotiations but also, in some important cases, for their changed character. More than previously, these negotiations dealt with problems that posed unprecedented worldwide threats. The Montreal Protocol, for example, had to meet the challenge of a potentially catastrophic global prospect: the deterioration of the stratospheric ozone layer. This challenge could be met only through urgent and coordinated action by all the major developed and developing countries. Climate change, with which we have yet to come to grips, is of this same nature.

The negotiations cited in this book called for a variety of approaches and negotiating strategies. They ranged from the decade-long series of exchanges with Canada on the acid rain problem to the single session in Sofia that resulted in wider cooperation on environmental issues among Cold War adversaries.

There were, however, shared elements among these negotiations that may provide useful lessons for future negotiators.

Managing the Interagency Process

Much of the most important work in reaching an international agreement takes place before a U.S. negotiator begins formal talks with his or her foreign counterparts. The negotiating strategy, including the degree of flexibility that will be given to the chief negotiator in reaching agreement, is worked out in an interagency process that is often contentious. This internal "negotiation" results in the preparation of negotiating guidance. Basic guidance is usually incorporated in the Circular 175 memorandum, a document through which the Department of State grants the authority to undertake the negotiation.

The same interagency group that manages the preparations for the negotiation often provides continuing direction to the negotiator as the talks proceed. It helps greatly if the U.S. negotiator is named early and is engaged throughout the interagency process. For example, I might not have been able to successfully complete the negotiation of the space station agreement, given the disagreements between the State Department and the Department of Defense, if I had not chaired the interagency group that was set up to guide the U.S. negotiating team during the negotiation.

The Role of the Department of State

Much of the U.S. government reflects a special concern with the views of various interest groups. The Commerce Department, for example, ensures that the perspective of the business community is taken into account. Environmentalists look to the Environmental Protection Agency to be sensitive to their point of view. The National Marine Fisheries Service, an agency within the Commerce Department, looks out for the interests of fishermen, as well as for the health of the fish stocks that they exploit. Some agencies relate to more than one domestic constituency. The Department of the Interior, for example, works closely both with conservationists and with those who make use of resources on public lands.

The Department of State, with its mandate for managing the foreign affairs of the United States, does not have a special relationship with any particular domestic sector. Thus, a negotiator from the State Department is institutionally in a good position to act as an honest broker in sorting out the various interests that other government departments and agencies bring to the interagency table. International negotiations on environment and science usually raise issues on which agency views differ. The chief U.S. negotiator needs to play a central role in efforts to resolve these interagency disagreements.

Critics of the State Department sometimes argue that it does have a bias—one that operates in favor of getting an agreement at any cost. This criticism is often based on a suspicion that international agreements limit U.S. sovereignty and freedom of action. This was the case during the negotiation of the space station agreement in the dispute between State and Defense over how to handle the issue of potential national security uses of the station. As a State Department negotiator, I operated from my conviction that reaching agreements to cooperate with other countries in dealing with transboundary and global issues is a constructive and useful thing to do.

The negotiations on both the space station and the U.S.-USSR basic sciences agreement resulted from presidential initiatives, reinforced at summit meetings with foreign leaders. In both cases, individuals involved in the interagency process raised concerns from the point of view of their agencies. It was my job as lead negotiator in those instances to find a way of responding to legitimate agency concerns while at the same time seeking to ensure that the president's initiative was not frustrated. In undertaking this task, a negotiator has to accept that he or she will occasionally be caught in crossfire between disputing agencies and subjected to sharp criticism.

The job of a negotiator does not end with the initialing of a draft agreement. After concluding a negotiation, a U.S. chief negotiator is responsible for leading the effort to have the agreement signed and ratified by the U.S. government. That is not always an easy task. For example, in the case of the driftnet negotiation with Japan, as chief negotiator I had to vigorously argue the merits of the agreement, noting the support of the affected fisheries interests, in the face of strong opposition from a then-powerful senior U.S. senator, Ted Stevens of Alaska.

Working with the Stakeholders

A U.S. negotiator needs to be sensitive to the concerns of all the interest groups that have a stake in the issues under consideration. The negotiator must listen carefully to the people affected by the negotiation, to their representatives in Congress, and to the NGOs that are their advocates. For example, keeping in close touch with both Alaskan fishermen and the concerned environmental NGOs proved critical in the case of the driftnet agreement with Japan. In another instance, the key to the successful completion of the Porcupine caribou agreement with Canada was having representatives of all the interested parties on the U.S. side involved in the decisive final negotiating session.

My NASA counterpart, Peggy Finarelli, and I met with concerned congressional staffers before and after every negotiating session on space station cooperation over a three-year period. These meetings gave us strong congressional support for the agreement that we finally achieved to proceed with this multibillion-dollar project.

Negotiating Approach

During the negotiations with foreign partners, I found it helpful to minimize the perception of an adversarial relationship. I tried to nurture the sense that the parties to the negotiation, notwithstanding their differing interests and perspectives, were working together to deal with an issue that concerned them all. In this regard, it was often useful to limit the number and length of plenary sessions, especially after the opening stages of a negotiation. Such formal sessions have a role in airing the views of all the participants at the beginning of a negotiation and in confirming that agreement has been reached at the end. However, overuse of plenary sessions tends to waste time and encourage counterproductive restatements of entering positions.

Informal working groups and side discussions among heads of delegation assist in creating a sense of common purpose among the participants in a negotiation. This approach was particularly effective in the final conferences that dealt with fishing in the Bering Sea Donut Hole. Also, informal exchanges can be helpful in setting the stage for negotiations, for example, as with the months-long initial talks that I had with Canada on "proposed elements of an agreement" before the actual negotiation of an air quality agreement began.

Sometimes a negotiating counterpart might be prepared to accept a certain result substantively, but for various reasons is uneasy about having the issue highlighted in the final agreement. In the space station negotiation, we dealt with this issue by having our understanding on national security uses of the station covered in a side letter between negotiators, rather than placed in the agreement itself.

In other instances, impasses arise over the decisionmaking rules that the parties would follow when implementing the agreement. The multistep procedure for making major decisions about the Bering Sea pollock fishery may appear complex, but the insertion of that procedure overcame a serious obstacle to the successful conclusion of a negotiation that we had been pursuing intensively for several years. In the negotiation of the Porcupine caribou agreement with Canada, we reached agreement by using a "double majority" approach, which would require majorities of both the Canadian and the U.S. members of the International Porcupine Caribou Board to agree to send recommendations to the two governments.

To achieve their purposes, environment and science agreements require continuing cooperation among the parties. Thus, a U.S. negotiator needs to be acutely aware of the priorities of the other countries involved in a negotiation. Countries will withdraw from agreements that they do not view as in their interest. Although sanctions for noncompliance—such as the Montreal Protocol's restrictions on trade in chlorofluorocarbons—can be helpful, the best assurance of compliance over time is the sense of the parties to an agreement that their concerns and interests have been adequately taken into account.

Science-Based Agreements

Agreements dealing with global environmental issues often must be concluded on the basis of incomplete and uncertain information to avoid waiting until environmental damage becomes irreversible. To conclude a viable environment or science agreement, all sides in a negotiation need to be convinced that the commitments being undertaken are based on sound science as it is understood at the time of the negotiation, while recognizing that in most instances the relevant scientific knowledge is still evolving.

The Montreal Protocol, which was aimed at reversing the depletion of the stratospheric ozone layer, provides the most compelling example of the importance of a flexible, science-based approach to negotiating such agreements. The parties to the Montreal Protocol set up a science committee to report to them on the adequacy of the initial steps taken to reduce emissions of ozone-depleting chemicals. Reports from this science committee to subsequent meetings of the parties, such as the 1990 London conference, led to commitments to further reductions and phase-outs of ozone-depleting substances, which are now arresting ozone layer deterioration. The driftnet agreement with Japan provides another example of setting up a process that incorporates commitments to review and revise agreement provisions on the basis of new information. Such agreements must not only make sense in light of the existing state of scientific knowledge but also include a process for the regular reevaluation of their provisions on the basis of new information.

To make the best use of available science, a negotiator needs access to sound scientific expertise and must make the effort to become as informed as possible. Fortunately, the U.S. specialized agencies, such as NASA, NSF, and EPA, have a wealth of scientific experts who can lend support to U.S. delegations to international negotiations. Expertise from the private sector is also readily accessible. Close working relationships need to be established between a negotiator and his or her scientific advisers.

U.S. Leadership

The United States played a less dominant role in the world at the time of these negotiations than was the case earlier in the post–World War II period. Nonetheless, other countries continued to look to the United States for leadership in meeting global environmental and scientific challenges. When the United States was among the leaders in recognizing and addressing a problem, the prospects were good for a successful negotiation.

The Montreal Protocol negotiation provides an example of the impact of U.S. leadership. Before the negotiation of the protocol, the United States was in the vanguard of those urging forceful measures to limit the production and use of CFCs, and we backed up our arguments by being among the first to unilaterally ban CFC use in most aerosols.

As a result of U.S. leadership, some other countries were moved to go beyond initially more restrained positions and agree to the strong first steps that we sought to deal with the problem of ozone layer depletion. Subsequently, at the London meeting dealing with amendments and adjustments to the protocol, U.S. leadership temporarily wavered over the issue of funding for the developing countries, and this almost led to the collapse of the Montreal Protocol process that the United States had been so instrumental in starting.

The issue of U.S. leadership remains critical in global science and environment agreements. The record is clear. When U.S. leadership falters, the prospects for success in such negotiations drop precipitously—which brings us to the Kyoto Protocol.

Kyoto: Lessons Not Learned

The 1997 Kyoto Protocol, which dealt with the issue of climate change, did not result in commitments to reduce carbon dioxide emissions that the United States has been prepared to accept and to ratify. Nor did the protocol include any such commitments by developing countries. Part of the problem, in my view, was that we failed to adequately take into account our experience in previous environment and science negotiations. For example, before the Kyoto meeting, a designated U.S. chief negotiator did not develop over time a productive dialogue with Congress and with the domestic groups that would be affected by the protocol.

The lack of a coherent strategy for working with Congress was an especially glaring omission. It was clear throughout the run-up to Kyoto that we faced a highly skeptical, if not hostile, congressional majority. Yet there was no sustained and determined effort to work with Congress to try to overcome this obstacle to successfully concluding an agreement. My experience in previous negotiations indicates that it is better to work closely with concerned domestic interest groups and Congress, even when they are initially opposed to what we are trying to accomplish.

In the case of the Kyoto Protocol, the United States sought to lead the development of a domestic policy through international negotiations. I am convinced that such an approach is almost always fruitless. In the case of acid rain, for example, the United States went through more than a decade of frustrating and inconclusive efforts to join with Canada in dealing with this problem. Before we could resolve this issue with Canada, however, we had to come together domestically and pass legislation calling for national reductions in emissions of acid rain precursors. Similarly, before we could successfully take part in the negotiation of the Montreal Protocol and its amendments, we had to reach a decision domestically on what we were prepared to do to reduce our own emissions of CFCs.

Although I had retired from the State Department several years earlier, I was asked in September 1997 to serve as a consultant to assist in the preparations for the Kyoto negotiations. My first memo, dated September 22, to Melinda Kimble, the acting assistant secretary in the Bureau of Oceans and International Environmental and Scientific Affairs, painted a gloomy picture of our prospects. I concluded, "It is hard to envision an achievable result in Kyoto which we would view as fully satisfactory."

In a preparatory meeting for Kyoto held in Berlin, the parties reached certain understandings on what they would seek to accomplish in Kyoto. The so-called Berlin Mandate called on all countries, including the developing countries, to advance the implementation of their existing commitments to reduce greenhouse gas emissions. "Existing commitments" referred to the framework agreement on climate change that both developed and developing countries signed in Rio de Janeiro in 1992. The Rio agreement, however, included no specific mandatory emissions reduction targets.

In Berlin, only the developed countries made a commitment that they would agree to specific reductions in carbon dioxide emissions at the Kyoto conference. The developing countries did not view the vague, general language in the mandate about the responsibilities of all countries as obligating them to take any particular actions to reduce their emissions. My memo to Kimble noted the problem created by the Berlin Mandate: "In Berlin, we clearly made a commitment on which we cannot deliver— mandatory reductions from a 1990 base in the early years of the next century, with no balancing mandatory obligations on the part of the developing countries."

Under Secretary of State for Global Affairs Tim Wirth, who had been supervising preparations for Kyoto, left government service several months before the Kyoto meeting. Under Secretary of State for Economic, Business, and Agricultural Affairs Stuart Eizenstat was then named to head the U.S. delegation in Kyoto. The U.S. negotiating team arrived with no clear instructions on what level of reduction of carbon dioxide emissions, if any, it could accept. The final reduction numbers were worked out in Kyoto in talks among representatives of the developed countries, and the levels varied from country to country.

It would be hard to make the case that the emissions reduction commitments were determined on the basis of the science involved or that they adequately took into account economic realities. In some cases, it was not clear how the countries concerned could meet their emissions reduction targets. Further, the developing countries made no specific commitments to reduce greenhouse gas emissions. The U.S. Senate had put down a marker in July 1997 in the Byrd-Hagel Resolution, which passed 95–0, that any agreement without such commitments by developing countries would be unacceptable.

At the United Nations Conference on Climate Change in Bali in December 2007, the United States signaled its intention to join in a worldwide effort to develop by 2012 a successor regime to the one put in place under the Kyoto Protocol. As the United States returns to global negotiations on climate change and prepares to take part in a meeting on the subject in Copenhagen in December 2009, we would be well advised to reflect on the lessons learned in other global environmental negotiations.

The Montreal Protocol provides a particularly useful precedent. This is true even though the climate change problem is much more complex and far-reaching than was the threat posed by substances that deplete the stratospheric ozone layer. Whereas the response to the threat to the ozone layer affected major industries and involved adjustment costs amounting to billions of dollars, addressing global warming effectively requires fundamentally rethinking our carbon-based societies and taking steps that will affect virtually every aspect of economic activity.

The workshops that the U.S. negotiating team on the Montreal Protocol held with the affected industries, for example, helped greatly in gaining their acceptance of the constraints to be imposed by the agreement. Although the target audience would neces- sarily be much broader, some comparable attempt to work with affected industries could be helpful as the United States reengages on climate change. Since the negotiation of the Kyoto Protocol, many major companies have, in fact, become more concerned about global warming and are considering how they can best respond to the threat that it poses.

In establishing science and economic committees that regularly reported their findings, the parties to the Montreal Protocol took a critical step. The parties considered those reports every couple of years and, on the basis of those reports, made changes to their commitments under the agreement. This continuing review-and-revise process was essential to the ultimate success of the Montreal Protocol in achieving its objectives.

The parties to the Kyoto Protocol have taken note of the outstanding work done by the Intergovernmental Panel on Climate Change, which was established in 1988 by the World Meteorological Organization and the United Nations Environment Programme. This panel, which involves the work of more than 2,000 scientists from more than 130 countries, shared the 2007 Nobel Peace Prize with former Vice President Al Gore. It is, however, a separate body, and not the Kyoto parties' own creature, whose findings the parties would be obligated to review periodically as a basis for considering modifications to their commitments under the agreement.

It was also significant that the Montreal Protocol, unlike the Kyoto Protocol, included a specific commitment by the developing countries to contribute to emissions cuts. Their reductions were to take place over a longer time than those of the developed countries and were expected to be accompanied by funding to assist them in phasing out ozone-depleting chemicals, as well as technology transfers from developed countries. The developing countries' acceptance of some specific requirements in addressing the problem of ozone depletion, even though they were weaker commitments, was critical to the successful completion of the negotiation of the Montreal Protocol.

A commitment to achieve some limit on carbon dioxide emissions from leading developing countries, particularly China and India, will be needed if the world community of nations is to deal effectively with the problem of climate change. However, developing countries remain strongly resistant to specific mandatory targets for reduced greenhouse gas emissions, fearing that their economic development will be undermined. A possible interim step might be to implement a "pledge and review" approach, whereby developing countries undertake to create and implement their own emissions limitation programs and agree to submit them for review and comment by other parties to an agreement.

Such an approach could be buttressed by commitments by developing countries to some particular goals, such as reaching a certain level of renewable energy use or an energy intensity target to reduce the amount of energy needed to achieve a given increase in gross domestic product. Any of these steps would need to be accompanied by assurances from developed countries of financial and technological assistance for accomplishing them.

Commitments from developing countries will probably not be forthcoming unless and until developed countries—particularly the United States—which have been most responsible for creating the problem of global warming, show greater leadership in mitigating it. The importance of having both the leadership of the principal developed countries and the full involvement of the major developing countries was shown in the 1990 London meeting of the parties to the Montreal Protocol. It was not until China and India decided to join the United States and the other major developed countries as parties to the protocol that the final breakthroughs were achieved, which put us on a path to reversing the deterioration of the stratospheric ozone layer.

Looking to the Future

In future high-priority negotiations on environment and science, including those on global warming, I believe that an essential first step is to designate an experienced chief negotiator early enough that he or she can play a central role in every phase of the negotiation. The negotiator needs to be fully involved, from the interagency preparation of negotiating guidelines to the signing and ratification of the negotiated agreement, and have a major responsibility for generating support within the U.S. government, including Congress, and in the private sector for the negotiation and the resulting agreement. It is encouraging that the Obama administration has named a climate change envoy, Todd Stern, who will be in a position to play this role with respect to negotiations on global warming.

The world will be facing some serious environment and science challenges in the years ahead. In addition to global warming, developments in such fields as nanotechnology and biotechnology will pose new problems. More will need to be done to limit emissions of individual pollutants, such as ground-level ozone and particulates. Desertification and the loss of tropical forests, biodiversity, and coral reefs will remain on the agenda. A continuing and alarming collapse of fisheries around the world will have to be addressed. Further, we will need to find ways to continue moving forward with cooperation on major science projects, such as space research, the development of fusion power, and advanced supercolliders. Moreover, we can be sure that other environment and science issues not now envisioned will arise.

In many cases, the challenges to be faced will require a coordinated multilateral response. On the basis of what has so far been accomplished, there are some grounds for optimism that those challenges can be met. I remain hopeful that with U.S. leadership, coming international negotiations on environment and science issues will yield positive results and contribute to the resolution of many troublesome global problems.

notes

Chapter 1. Earth's Ozone Shield

1. Philip Shabecoff, "Consensus on the Threat to the Ozone," *New York Times*, December 7, 1986.
2. Ibid.
3. Richard Elliot Benedick, *Ozone Diplomacy: New Directions in Safeguarding the Planet*, rev. ed. (Cambridge, MA: Harvard University Press, 1998). Benedick's book includes a comprehensive review of events, domestic and international, leading up to the conclusion of the negotiation of the Montreal Protocol.
4. Cass Peterson, "Administration Ozone Policy May Favor Sunglasses, Hats: Support for Chemical Cutbacks Reviewed," *The Washington Post*, May 29, 1987.
5. Herblock editorial cartoon, *The Washington Post*, June 3, 1987.
6. Peterson, "Administration Ozone Policy May Favor Sunglasses, Hats."
7. Philip Shabecoff, "U.S. Urged to End Opposition to Ozone Aid," *New York Times*, June 13, 1990.
8. 8. Michael Weisskopf, "United States Drops Opposition to CFC Phaseout Fund: Business, Foreign Leaders Had Urged Reversal," Washington Post, June 16, 1990.
9. Claiborne Pell, "CFC Fund Decision Showed Flaws in US Policymaking," *Christian Science Monitor*, June 22, 1990.
10. Ibid.
11. Richard J. Smith cable to Counselor Robert Zoellick et al., unclassified cable number 12295, section 2, para. IV from American

Embassy London to Secretary of State, Washington, DC, June 25, 1990.

12. John Sununu, as quoted in Weisskopf, "United States Drops Opposition to CFC Phaseout Fund."

13. "An Environmental Feat," *The Washington Post*, July 6, 1990.

Chapter 2. The Driftnet Dilemma

1. International waters, referred to as the high seas, are those beyond 200 miles of any country's coastline.

2. The 200-mile exclusive economic zone (EEZ) is an area within which the coastal state controls and regulates the use of ocean resources.

3. Specifically, section 8 of the Fisherman's Protective Act, 22 U.S.C. 1978.

4. INPFC was established by agreement among the United States, Canada, and Japan for the purpose of coordinating research and making recommendations to their governments on anadromous species, such as salmon, in the North Pacific Ocean and the Bering Sea. (Anadromous fish spend their adult lives in the sea, but swim up rivers to spawn in fresh water.) The agreement, in the form of a protocol amending the Convention for the High Seas Fisheries of the North Pacific Ocean, entered into force in 1979.

5. All the excerpts below are taken from the draft of the testimony sent to me by the Senate Commerce Committee after my appearance before them. They may differ slightly from the version later published in the Congressional Record.

6. U.S. Embassy Tokyo unclassified cable number 2552 with subject line *US-Japan Driftnet Fisheries Agreement,* dated May 10, 1989. The excerpts are taken from paragraphs 1 and 4, respectively.

7. NOAA Press Release, June 29, 1989, *Mosbacher Announces Agreement on Monitoring Pacific Fish Catch.*

8. Linda M. B. Paul, online document, "The 1989 North Pacific Joint Observer Program, Results," in *High Seas Driftnetting: The Plunder of the Global Commons—A Compendium,* rev. ed. (Kailua, HI: EarthTrust, 1994). www.earthtrust.org/dnpaper/npac.html#anchor1003632. Accessed June 2009.

9. U.S. Embassy Tokyo unclassified cable number 11631 with subject line *US-Japan Driftnet Agreement,* dated July 1, 1989.

Chapter 3. Acid Rains on Canadian-U.S. Relations

1. A White House statement on acid rain issued on March 19, 1986, noted that approximately $75 billion had been spent on reducing

emissions of acid rain precursors since the passage of the Clean Air Act Amendments of 1970.

2. According to a March 19, 1986, White House statement on acid rain, the United States had allocated $2.2 billion in research funds from fiscal year 1981 through fiscal year 1986 to develop clean coal technologies.

3. G-7 economic summit meetings—now, with the addition of Russia, G-8—are held annually among the leaders of the major industrialized countries: United States, Canada, United Kingdom, Germany, France, Italy, Japan, and Russia.

4. Alan Nixon and Thomas Curran, online document, "Chronology, 16 July 1990," in *Acid Rain*, 79-37E, Government of Canada, Parliamentary Research Branch, 1998, rev., dsp-psd.communication.gc.ca/Pilot/LoPBdP/CIR/7937-e.htm#CHRONOLOGY. Accessed July 2009.

5. Quoted from press release by Environment Canada (Ottawa) on the joint statement by de Cotret and Reilly, July 16, 1990, from author's personal files.

6. Richard Smith and Susan Biniaz, "Beyond Dispute: An Air Quality Agreement in the Context of a Consultative Relationship," *Canada–United States Law Journal* 17 (1991): 421–29, Case Western Reserve University.

7. Introduction to the "United States–Canada Air Quality Agreement: Progress Report 2006" (Washington, DC: U.S. Environmental Protection Agency, 2006), vii. www.epa.gov/airmarkt/progsregs/usca/docs/2006report.pdf. Accessed July 2009.

8. Ibid., viii.

Chapter 4. Caribou in the Oil Patch

1. Under Section 1002 of the Alaska National Interest Lands Conservation Act (ANILCA) of 1980, a part of the northern coast of ANWR was set aside for study about whether oil and gas development should take place there. The calving grounds of the Porcupine caribou are located primarily within the Section 1002 area.

Chapter 5. The U.S.-USSR Science Agreement

1. Initialing an agreed text may be used to mark the completion of a negotiation. The subsequent signing of the agreement by an authorized representative of a government may by itself bring an agreement into force if no further domestic action needs to be taken. In other circumstances, signature may indicate the government's intent to pursue the domestic procedures necessary for the

agreement to enter into force. For example, in the United States, treaties require domestic action after signature (namely, the advice and consent of the U.S. Senate given by a two-thirds favorable vote). In this instance, however, the commitments by the United States and the Soviet Union were in the form of an executive agreement, which would enter into force upon signature.

2. Gene Grabowski, "Scientific Agreement Terms Favor Soviets, Worried Officials Charge," the *Washington Times*, May 16, 1988.

Chapter 6. The Space Station Partnership

1. David Sanger, "Weinberger Letter on Allies' Role in Space Station Stirs Furor," *New York Times*, April 10, 1987.

Chapter 7. Human Rights and the Environment

1. At a meeting of heads of state in Paris in 1990, steps were launched to institutionalize CSCE and shape it to meet the challenges of the post–Cold War era. On January 1, 1995, the Organization for Security and Co-operation in Europe (OSCE) was established as a successor organization. It has since played an important and expanding role in undertaking activities related to conflict prevention, security, and human rights. It has, for example, been active in monitoring elections.

2. Ecoglasnost took its name from the Russian word *glasnost,* a policy of openness, which was being used by the reformist leader Gorbachev to describe his new approach in the Soviet Union. Thus, the group's name could be read as a call for ecological openness.

3. James Baker, "Diplomacy for the Environment," an address before the National Governors Association in Washington, DC, February 26, 1990, reprinted in the *U.S. Department of State Dispatch* 1(1), September 3, 1990.

Chapter 8. Fishing in the Donut Hole

1. The Aleutian Basin includes the Donut Hole and much of the surrounding Bering Sea. The Donut Hole makes up 19 percent of the Aleutian Basin and 10 percent of the entire Bering Sea.

2. David A. Balton, "The Bering Sea Doughnut Hole Convention: Regional Solution, Global Implications," in *Governing High Seas Fisheries: Interplay of Global and Regional Regimes*, Olav Shram Stokked. 146 (Oxford University Press, 2001).

3. The Law of the Sea Convention was completed in 1982 and received the required number of ratifications to come into force

in 1994. U.S. ratification is still awaiting the advice and consent of the Senate.

4. The pollock catch in the Donut Hole in 1985 totaled approximately 364,000 metric tons.

5. Such a convention would be in the form of a treaty, which would involve binding international commitments. In the United States, ratification of a treaty requires obtaining the consent of the Senate by a two-thirds favorable vote.

6. When the Russian Federation replaced the Soviet Union in the Donut Hole negotiations, the head of the Soviet delegation, Dr. V. K. Zilanov, remained in place to become the head of the Russian delegation.

7. Balton, "Bering Sea Doughnut Hole Convention," 166–71. Balton discusses in some detail the interplay among the Donut Hole agreement, the provisions of the Law of the Sea Convention, and other efforts to deal with high-seas fisheries and fish stocks that straddle international waters and coastal states' EEZs.

index